THE RYMAN REMEMBERS

RECIPES & RECOLLECTIONS
THE RYMAN AUDITORIUM

FRP

Nashville, Tennessee

To order additional copies, please call or write FRP™

Copyright © 1996 by FRP™
Publishing division of Southwestern/Great American, Inc.
P. O. Box 305142, Nashville, Tennessee 37230
1-800-358-0560

Conceived, edited, and published under the direction of:

Ralph Mosley   Chairman of the Board
Tom McDow   President and Publisher
Dave Kempf   Division Vice President and
                                 Executive Editor

The Ryman Remembers

Managing Editor   Mary Cummings
Project Editor and Research   Jane Hinshaw
Contributing Editor   Dixie Hall
Essayist   Beth Stein

Book and Jacket Design   Starletta Polster
Art Director   Steve Newman
Production   Mark Sloan

A **GAYLORD ENTERTAINMENT** COMPANY

116 5th Avenue North, Nashville, Tennessee 37219
615-254-1445
Project Coordinator   David French
Assistant Project Coordinator   Trish McGee

The Ryman Remembers: Recipes & Recollections, The Ryman Auditorium.
         p.   cm.
   Includes index.
   ISBN 0-87197-449-5
   1. Cookery.   2. Ryman Auditorium (Nashville, Tenn.)—History.
I. Favorite Recipes Press.
TX714.R95   1996
641.5—dc20
                                                        96-33463
                                                            CIP

Manufactured in the United States of America
First Printing: 1996

Dedication

About this old church, she said...

Precious songs unto me have my children sang
Closely guarded inside my heart, such joy they always bring
In the midflight of December's past when I was forgotten and
    lamps burned low
It was on this rock on which I stand for my strength I had to go.

On a foundation as pure as God's own breath, I have stood the
    test of time
Now beyond a shadow of anyone's doubt, I have not been
    left behind
I grew tired and I grew weary in you, *that* I will confide
But never for a moment did I forget you, my arms were always
    open wide.

I am but a diamond that has been covered up in dust
Or like a precious metal that's been paralyzed by rust
Now I return triumphant, again I have been found
Always and forever, I am the Queen of this town.

So, sing me a song as sad as Hank
Have Bill Monroe yodel twice
Get Minnie Pearl to pull some pranks
Or have the Old Judge to read something nice
DeFord come and blow your harp and make that baby cry
Because Uncle Dave's coming in on the Woodbury bus as
    our redemption draweth nigh
Nigh and nearer, "Nearer My God To Thee," have Roy Acuff sing
While Maybelle plays her auto harp
My children know how to make the rafters ring.

Marty Stuart offers the perfect metaphor for celebrating the Ryman, old and new, as he himself has been called the past, present, and future of country music. The traditional roots of his music run deep and wide, beginning as a teenager performing with Lester Flatt, but he is as progressive an artist as any who appear on the Ryman's stage today.

Photograph courtesy of
Donnie Beauchamp

Marty first appeared on the Ryman stage as a thirteen-year-old mandolin player, and has gone on to win a Country Music Association Award and a Grammy. He says that his biggest moment is still his induction into the Grand Ole Opry.

Now, new melodies drift up out of my windows
That bloom like magnolias in the night
Sent by young and fearless hearts
Grandchildren filled with light
Chosen and committed, hands firm upon the plow
Knowing well from whence they came
Beholding the future like it was now.

So, hit those low notes Randy Travis
Make way for Alison Krauss
Tell Travis and Marty to turn it down easy
Be reverent when they rock this house
Clint Black, come and blow your harp and make that baby cry
Because Gill, Garth and Jackson are bringing it home as we
    kiss this century good-bye.

To the dignified and different, sinners and saints
Come feast on the sounds and the sights
A natural wonder for all to behold
We're the reason God made Saturday night.

—*Marty Stuart*

Contents

*Will Campbell is a
well-known writer,
lecturer, and humorist;
he has also been, at
various times, a soldier,
university chaplain,
civil rights activist,
itinerant social worker,
farmer, tour bus cook
for his friend Waylon
Jennings, and self-
styled reprobate. His
book,* Brother to a
Dragonfly, *was listed
by the* New York
Times *as one of the
year's best books in 1977.*
Time *magazine reported
it as one of ten books
of the decade
predicted to survive.*

Foreword

Back in 1992 Roger Miller died. He was too young to go but we transients on earth don't make those decisions. Roger wanted his memorial service to be in the old Ryman where he had started his career and soared to success and fame.

There was a problem. Since 1974 when the Grand Ole Opry moved to its present location the Ryman had lain fallow. Except for an occasional tour she had stood as a lonely relic, her past glory of fiddles, banjos, guitars and harmonicas ringing only in memories of the past. Where once laughter and applause prevailed there was now the musty smell of antiquity, the Captain's lady herself standing silently sad. But yet proud. Fire codes prevented more than a few to gather inside. She was a forlorn lady on Fifth Avenue North; one more street person depending on the kindness of strangers.

Still that was where Roger Miller wanted his remembering friends to gather. And so we did. An exception was made for the occasion. The gloom of silence stepped aside, making way for hundreds of Roger's friends and colleagues to mourn, tell Roger stories, sing Roger songs, laugh, all in celebration of the life of a great man in a great place. Waylon, Kris, Marty, Chet, Mel, son Dean. Singing and testifying. From as near as Sixteenth Avenue and as far away as New York, New Haven and Tokyo they had convened. A tribute to Roger Miller. A tribute to Captain Ryman's legacy.

This would be the last gig in the old Ryman. It was November. Fall. A time of ending. There had been rumors that the old building would be torn down. Those gathered that evening knew better. They were standing on sacred ground and things holy cannot be destroyed. Even if the body were destroyed the soul would march on. They had all stood on this stage before. In the minds and hearts of millions the Ryman would endure.

It was not long until an announcement was made that the Ryman Auditorium was to be renovated and used regularly for important concerts and occasions. A resurrection.

Almost two years after Roger died Trisha Yearwood called and asked me to marry her. Said she wanted to get married in the Ryman. She said the wedding would be the very first event in the newly renovated Ryman Auditorium. That was 1994.

I told her I thought it was appropriate for a rising young star to get married in what has become the cathedral of every country picker in the universe. Even more fitting for a wedding ceremony to be the first occasion in the new Ryman since originally it had been a place for revival meetings, and weddings are a sort of reviving of two people.

"Then you'll do it," Trisha said. She sounded happy and excited.

"Do what?" I teased, feigning seriousness.

"Marry me."

I wanted to phrase my answer in a way that would not hurt her feelings. Artists are so sensitive you know. "Now I don't want to offend you, Miss Yearwood," I began slowly. "You are a beautiful woman and I love your music. But I'm an old man now and you're so young and elegant." I hesitated when she didn't respond. "Plus, I have a delicate problem when it comes to being the one to marry you." Her silence continued and I could tell I wasn't doing too well. But I went on. "Miss Yearwood, I'm already married to another woman. And

Brother to a Dragonfly was also a finalist for the National Book Award and won the Lillian Smith Prize. Glad River, a novel, won the Friends of American Writers Award. His collective works were awarded the Lyndhurst Prize. He was the subject of historian Thomas Connelly's Will Campbell and the Soul of the South and the first recipient of the Alex Haley Award for Distinguished Tennessee Writers.

come next January I will have been married to her for fifty years. Our children have planned this big party and I'm afraid neither Brenda nor the children would look kindly on my simply…"

Campbell's most recent published work, The Stem of Jesse, *details the events leading up to the admittance of the first black student to Mercer University.*

"No, no, no," Trisha interrupted. She laughed lightly but still sounded uncomfortable. "I'm not proposing to you. I'm just asking you to marry me."

"Well. Uh."

"You know. Perform the ceremony."

"Oh," I said.

Then she told me her fiancé was a fellow named Robert Reynolds, that he was handsome, a fine musician, was a member of The Mavericks, that she was very much in love with him and if I would do the ceremony in the new Ryman she was sure they would have a long and happy life together. We both laughed then.

It was such a lovely wedding. It was May. Springtime. When flowers are proclaiming their beauty, birds are singing their own songs of love, and all the beasties of the fields and forests are chasing and cavorting in their own mode of love, courtship and marriage. Spring: a time of new beginnings.

At the rehearsal we discovered that the renovating of the Ryman was not quite complete. While we were on stage the workers were scurrying around, putting finishing touches here, correcting things not quite right there. That pleased me for it gave me an opening for a little homily, a chance to say that marriage is like that — never quite finished, always requiring a little touching up, correcting mistakes, ever trying to get all things right but not giving up when we don't. Even after fifty years.

Then I told them that marriage was the antidote for personal loneliness, and if they wanted to know what real loneliness was like just hum or sing a few bars of a song that had been sung on the Ryman stage many times: Hank Williams' "I'm So Lonesome I Could Cry." Then I had them sing the words of "Amazing Grace" to the tune of "I'm So Lonesome I Could Cry." Lyrics of joy and hope sung to a melody of solitude. The old Ryman had been lonely for years. Trisha and Robert cheered her up.

"First to last" whispers of sadness. "Last to first" has a gladdening, triumphal ring of victory. Roger left us in the fall and wanted his memorial to be the last performance in the Old Ryman. Trisha and Robert were married in the spring and wanted to be first in the New.

"The new is but the old come true."
                                                      —Will Campbell

The Ryman was a church before it was the Mother Church of Country Music, so we thought it was the perfect place to blend the spiritual side with the music.
                            —Trisha Yearwood

Preface

At first glance, the Ryman Auditorium might seem like odd company for a cookbook.

Tracing the rich and colorful history of this building and listening to the many fascinating stories its walls can tell, however, you realize this renowned piece of architecture is not unlike a fine recipe itself. From its beginnings in 1885 as the personal mission of converted riverboat captain Tom Ryman, who wanted a grand hall for revivals, to its current success as Nashville's most cherished theater, the tabernacle has been called a collection of widely diverse ingredients mixed all together.

The history of "The Mother Church of Country Music" is as rich and eclectic a concoction as you'll find anywhere. As any good cook knows, sometimes the strangest ingredients produce the most delectable results.

In the case of the Ryman, it's a sweet tale indeed.

Of course, the Ryman is best known as a former home of the Grand Ole Opry and most closely associated with country music. Yet, the diversity of the tabernacle's history may surprise you. Long before bluegrass and country bands struck their first twangy chords in this building, Edward Strauss and the Vienna Orchestra and the finest symphonies from New York, Chicago, and Boston played the Ryman. The great tenor Enrico Caruso sang opera here, and Isadora Duncan, Anna Pavlova, Martha Graham, Nijinsky, and the Ballet Russe all danced across its wooden stage. Scholars and presidents delivered speeches, John Philip Sousa's U.S. Marine Corps Band romped through its famous marches, and Sarah Bernhardt performed her renowned "Camille." From Charlie Chaplin to Katharine Hepburn, American explorer Robert Edwin Peary to Trigger, prize fights to ice shows, the Ryman has seen it all through the years.

And then there is that little thing called the Grand Ole Opry. Beginning in 1943, the Ryman became home to the Opry, which had quickly outgrown several smaller venues. Over the next thirty years, the tabernacle stage would serve up all the legends of country music — and then some. Hank Williams, Minnie Pearl, Roy Acuff, Loretta Lynn, George Jones and Tammy Wynette, Kitty Wells, Eddy Arnold, Johnny Cash, Elvis Presley, and many, many more would all feel those wide boards beneath their boots, and look out over the semicircular hall filled with the eager faces of fans.

Many veterans of the Grand Ole Opry look back on the Ryman days as the Opry's sweetest. Despite its lack of dressing areas, air conditioning and other accommodations, the musty old hall held a magic for performers and fans alike. Something about being jammed in there all together, under less than ideal circumstances, gave rise to a sense of family, fun, and celebration, as well as special friendships.

DeFord Bailey

The Opry stayed at the Ryman until March 15, 1974 — its last Friday night performance there. On Saturday, the renowned radio show made its debut in its brand new, state-of-the-art auditorium, the Opry House, inside the Opryland USA theme park complex.

Although by now age and decay had taken over the Ryman, her memories were still clear. During that last performance, performers paid moving tributes to the old building that had been home for more than thirty years. Many of them wept on stage, remembering all the good times there.

The show closed officially when George Morgan, the Four Guys, Ray Pillow, Lonzo and Oscar, and Ernie Ashworth had performed that night. But after the radio announcer signed off the air, Johnny and June Carter Cash came out to lead an old-fashioned gospel sing in the finest tradition of the Ryman's roots. Hymns were sung and praises lifted once more inside the old hallowed hall, ending with

Photograph courtesy of Grand Ole Opry Archives

11

a rousing rendition of "Will The Circle Be Unbroken?" And one final "Amen."

During the Opry years, the Ryman had continued to host a variety of entertainment, from Broadway productions to television tapings to symphony. But when the Opry moved out, it signaled the end of life as the Ryman had known it. Aside from an occasional special event, such as the one in 1991 when Emmylou Harris and the Nash Ramblers recorded an album there, and in 1992 when the building's 100th birthday was celebrated, the old building stood empty for almost two decades. The only voices were those of tourists who paid a nominal fee to stroll its creaky aisles and imagine what this dilapidated hall must have been like in its heyday.

One plan called for the Ryman to be torn down and the bricks used to build a chapel on the now-thriving Opryland USA property. But historic preservationists and longtime Nashvillians who loved the old building were determined not to lose the architectural treasure. Even the costs of bringing the Ryman up to codes standards, however, were discouraging.

But, in April of 1993, Gaylord Entertainment — the company that developed the Opryland USA theme park and hotel complex among other things — announced it would renovate the Ryman to its former glory and reopen it as an entertainment venue. You could feel the joy, pride, and relief that ran through the community, as headlines foretold plans for the much-loved Ryman.

That renovation was completed in June of 1994, when the Ryman opened once again as a thriving theater. The careful restoration had lovingly maintained the tabernacle's remarkable character, but also added the accommodations today's performers and audiences expect. It has been heralded by preservationists, technicians, artists, and visitors as a resounding success.

The Ryman continues to flourish as Nashville's most beloved venue. The big names of country, both young and old, as well as an eclectic collection of other artists, have performed from its newly polished stage. They all love the Ryman. They're in awe of its acoustics and cherish the intimacy between performer and audience it affords. During John Prine's 1996 concert there, the legendary singer-songwriter paused briefly in the middle of a rousing, energetic show. He stepped to the edge of the Ryman stage and simply took a moment to survey the sea of fans that surrounded him from front row to back balcony. Drinking in the magic of what it's like to play in this magnificent hall, Prine nodded reflectively, then grinned. Many a performer has done the same thing.

The Ryman Centennial Celebration included such stars as Sam Bush, Ricky Skaggs, Connie Smith, Bill Monroe, Emmylou Harris and Vince Gill.

"The Ryman remains the most amazing place I've ever sung in," Vince Gill told *USA Today.* "The acoustics, the way the music reverberates and decays, is so perfect.... The first time I sang there, the heat went all through my body when I started singing. It was definitely a spiritual vibe, an awesome feeling."

Pop/Christian artist and longtime Nashville resident Amy Grant perhaps said it best: "I have dreamed of singing on this stage. How wonderful to be a part of a place that honors not only where we are going — who we are becoming — but celebrates where we have been and all that we come from."

MOTHER
CHURCH

...THE UNBROKEN CIRCLE

It's a cold February night in 1995. The Ryman is bubbling with excitement as the first Nashville Music Awards gets under way. Musicians, songwriters, executives from the business community and music industry, and fans have all gathered here to celebrate the broad diversity of music represented in Nashville today.

Midway through the show, the curtains open to reveal six young men in neon-colored suits. As their loud and erratic electric music begins, the band members fling themselves about the newly renovated Ryman stage as the front man screams lyrics into a microphone.

The band is the Newsboys, up-and-coming rockers on the Christian music scene.

An older gentleman in the audience, familiar with the Ryman's gentler, more conservative roots, chuckles that such a raucous display was likely a first for this hallowed old hall.

How wrong he is.

The Newsboys probably have more in common with the Ryman's earliest days than most of the acts that have graced that stage since. Their loud, confrontational approach to spreading the Christian message is precisely how the Ryman came into existence.

The year was 1885. Horses and buggies rattled over the cobblestones of downtown Nashville as a huge crowd gathered beneath a sprawling tent. The draw was Sam Jones, a Georgia preacher famous for his fire-and-brimstone brand of evangelism.

Just down the road from there, the riverfront played host to a different breed of folks. The rowdies and roustabouts who hung around there frequently had their fun by barging in on these revivals and heckling the preacher. Riverboat captain Tom Ryman was sometimes among the instigators.

But legend has it that on this particular evening, as Ryman and his buddies were beginning their usual mischief, Ryman began to listen to Jones' sermon. As he listened, he realized that Jones was talking about something as sacred to the captain as the river itself: mother.

When I get up to preach, I just knock out the bung and let nature cut her capers.

—Sam Jones

The Union Gospel Tabernacle with its central pulpit
Photograph courtesy of Ryman Archives

The polished wooden

pews sat glistening

in the afternoon sun

that filtered through

the windows and gave

the aroma of a

thousand old guitars.

There's nothing

else like it. It makes

you hungry

for good music.

—Tom T. Hall

Thereafter, Tom Ryman became one of Jones' most ardent converts. The enlightened riverboat captain threw himself into a campaign to build a tabernacle where Jones could spread the almighty gospel to thousands at a time. He envisioned a grand auditorium and selected architect Hugh C. Thompson to design it. Ryman gave huge sums of his own money to the project and led the charge to inspire others to do the same.

Construction began on the Union Gospel Tabernacle in 1889. It was to be used in a manner "strictly religious, nonsectarian and nondenominational, and for the purpose of promoting religion, morality, and the elevation of humanity to a higher plane and more usefulness." One year later, Jones delivered his first sermon there, but the auditorium was far from completed. Finishing it out proved to be a daunting task. Despite their best efforts, Jones and Ryman struggled to keep the project financed.

An interesting challenge came in 1897. Coinciding with the Tennessee Centennial Exposition, the Confederate Veterans Association promised to bring Nashville the biggest convention it had ever seen, if the Tabernacle could house the meetings. To seat all the veterans, they needed to build the balcony — or "gallery" as it was called — which was part of architect Hugh Thompson's original plan.

Jones, once again, set to plying the guilt-ridden and promising salvation, all the while encouraging the repentant to contribute to the Tabernacle's building fund. On a shoestring, a prayer, and a very tight schedule, Ryman and Jones managed to finance the formidable and sturdy gallery in time for the convention.

At that point, the auditorium was pretty much as you see it now, except the stage was not yet built. It seated 3,755 people and had cost about $100,000 to build, an exorbitant sum in that day.

Ryman died three years later in 1904. His funeral took place on Christmas Day at the Tabernacle, with Sam Jones officiating. Some 4,000 mourners filled the old wooden pews, as Jones talked of the captain's devotion to the very building in which they now gathered. Right then and there, Jones proposed changing the Tabernacle's name to Ryman Auditorium and asked that mourners signify their approval by

standing. Collectively, every man, woman, and child rose in tribute.

The Ryman rose up for the sake of religion, and religion remains the one constant throughout. From those first tent revivals in the late 1890s to the sounds of current contemporary Christian artists, the Ryman has been filled with a hunger for the spiritual and songs of the soul.

Through the years, evangelist Billy Sunday and religious crusaders such as Aimee Semple McPherson, Gipsy Smith, and Norman Vincent Peale would preach the gospel there.

The heavenly sounds of Fisk University's Jubilee Singers frequently filled the hall, and, beginning in the late forties, all-night gospel sings rang to the rafters regularly.

It was the gospel that gave birth to the Ryman and the gospel that closed it down in 1974, with Johnny and June Carter Cash leading the Ryman's last Opry gathering in "Will The Circle Be Unbroken." Followed by a quiet "Amen."

Although the Ryman's affiliation with religious and moral certitude waned over the years, there have certainly been many highlights past and present that would have made Captain Tom Ryman proud. Even when the Ryman began booking all sorts of entertainment, it continued to be a favorite gathering place for church groups and religious conventions. It has assumed the role of the church for Ryman's funeral and Roger Miller's memorial service, as well as for the marriages of Opry member Brother Oswald and country stars Trisha Yearwood and Robert Reynolds of The Mavericks in May of 1994.

The religious tradition continues today as Nashville's thriving Christian artists often make the Ryman their choice. "Sam's Place," a Sunday night inspirational show hosted by Gary Chapman, has become one of Nashville's hottest tickets. It gathers some of the biggest names in the business — Wynonna, Steven Curtis Chapman, Amy Grant, CeCe Winans, Michael W. Smith — for an informal evening of gospel singing, audience participation, laughter, and celebration.

Amen.

When you leave the Grand Ole Opry you should be able to say to yourself that you got some good out of it, that it was maybe like going to a good church service.

—Roy Acuff

The story of the Ryman Auditorium actually begins in a tent, where the controversial evangelist Sam Jones of Georgia was holding revival meetings in Nashville in 1885. Converted from his early days of dissipation by a deathbed promise to his father in 1872, he became an itinerant preacher and was commanding crowds of 8,000 to 10,000 by the time he began preaching in Nashville. He was criticized as coarse and even obscene, but was proud of the fact that he called "a spade a spade and a hog a hog" and claimed that "When I get up to preach, I just knock out the bung and let nature cut her capers."

Scripture Cake

Young Sam Jones' grandmother, who took care of him as a boy, might easily have introduced him to this cake. She was reputed to have read the Bible through thirty-seven times on her knees. "And he looked, and, behold, there was a cake baked on the coals and a cruse of water at his head. And he did eat and drink, and laid him down again." (I Kings 19:6)

Samuel Porter Jones

1 cup butter, softened (Judges 5:25)
2 cups sugar (Jeremiah 6:20)
2 tablespoons honey (I Samuel 14:25, Isaiah 7:15)
6 eggs (Jeremiah 17:11)
4½ cups flour (I Kings 4:22)
2 teaspoons baking powder (Amos 4:5)
1 teaspoon salt (Leviticus 2:13)
½ teaspoon each nutmeg, allspice and cinnamon (II Chronicles 9:9, Solomon 4:14-16)
½ cup milk (Judges 4:19)
2 cups raisins (I Samuel 30:12)
2 cups dried figs (Nahum 3:12)
2 cups chopped almonds (Numbers 17:8)

Cream the butter, sugar and honey in a bowl until light and fluffy. Beat in the eggs 1 at a time. Add a mixture of the dry ingredients alternately with the milk, mixing well after each addition. Stir in the raisins, figs and almonds. Spoon into a greased and floured tube pan. Bake at 325 degrees for 40 minutes. Cool in the pan for 10 minutes and invert onto a serving plate to cool completely.

Yield: 16 servings.

Grape Jelly

As a child, Louise Ryman Buchanan Proctor, granddaughter of Thomas Ryman, spent many summers at the Ryman home on Rutledge Hill. In a 1981 letter, she described the home and an outbuilding of substantial red brick, chimney at either end, and a rooftop embellished with iron lacework. She remembered fondly the arbor from the house to this outbuilding, covered with Concord grapes in season.

Thomas Green Ryman

> *2 quarts slightly underripe young*
>   *Concord grapes*
> *2 cups water*
> *2 apples, peeled, cut into quarters*
> *⅓ cup vinegar*
> *1 (1-inch) cinnamon stick*
> *1 teaspoon whole cloves*
> *8 cups sugar*

Crush the grapes with the water in a saucepan. Add the apples, vinegar, cinnamon, cloves and sugar. Bring to a boil gradually, stirring to dissolve the sugar.

Cook until the grapes are tender and the mixture is thickened, stirring frequently. Strain into hot sterilized jars, leaving ½ inch headspace; seal with 2-piece lids.

Yield: about 5 pints.

Thomas Green Ryman was a prosperous owner of a line of steamboats and a saloon on Broad Street in 1885 when he converted to a life of good works, civic virtue and gospel evangelism at Sam Jones' tent meeting. That very night he discussed with Jones the need for a "Tabernacle for all denominations" and legend has it that Ryman went directly back to his saloon and began pouring barrels of whiskey into the Cumberland River, ordering all of his steamboats up and down the river to do the same. Ryman was responsible for raising most of the money to build the Union Gospel Tabernacle later renamed for him.

The original design of the Union Gospel Tabernacle

Architecturally, the Tabernacle recalls the tent meetings it replaced, with its broad peak rising one hundred feet from the ground, and its ecclesiastical character most evident in the great circle of its interior, where the pews, originally circled around the pulpit, are bathed in the warm lights from the stained glass windows. Current Ryman manager Steve Buchanan thinks that the windows are one of the reasons that the Auditorium has such an impact on performers. "They look up from the stage and see those windows and the light coming in, and it's like no other place they've played."

Sunday Fried Chicken and Gravy

Fried chicken has long been the mainstay of any Sunday dinner or revival meeting in the South and continues to be a favorite. Just remove the skin to appeal to more health-conscious modern palates, but don't skimp on the pepper.

> 1 chicken, cut up
> 2 cups flour
> Salt and pepper to taste
> Vegetable oil for frying
> 2 cups buttermilk
> 3 cups milk

Rinse the chicken and pat dry, discarding the skin if desired. Mix the flour, salt and pepper in a bowl. Preheat the oil in a heavy Dutch oven or deep cast-iron skillet. Dip the chicken in the buttermilk and coat well with the flour, reserving the remaining flour mixture. Fry in the heated oil until golden brown on all sides. Drain on paper towels.

Pour off most of the oil in the skillet. Sift several tablespoons of the reserved flour mixture into the reserved drippings. Cook until golden brown, stirring constantly. Stir in the milk. Cook until thickened, stirring constantly. Serve with the chicken, mashed potatoes and biscuits.

Yield: 5 servings.

Sunday Devil's Food Cake

1 tablespoon vinegar
1 cup milk
2 cups sugar
2 eggs
2½ cups flour
2 teaspoons baking soda
½ teaspoon salt
1 cup margarine, softened
1 teaspoon vanilla extract
½ cup baking cocoa
1 cup boiling water
6 tablespoons margarine
6 tablespoons milk
1½ cups sugar
½ cup chocolate chips

Stir the vinegar into 1 cup milk in a small bowl and let stand. Combine 2 cups sugar, eggs, flour, baking soda, salt, 1 cup margarine, vanilla and baking cocoa in a large mixer bowl and mix well. Add the boiling water and mix well. Spoon into a greased 9x13-inch cake pan.

Bake at 350 degrees for 40 to 45 minutes or until a wooden pick inserted in the cake comes out clean. Combine 6 tablespoons margarine, 6 tablespoons milk and 1½ cups sugar in a saucepan and mix well. Bring to a boil, stirring constantly. Cook for 2 minutes, stirring constantly; remove from the heat. Stir in the chocolate chips until melted. Spread on the cake.

Yield: 15 servings.

The well-known preacher Billy Sunday held several revival meetings in the Auditorium in the twenties and thirties. Jack Norman, Sr., relates the time when Reverend Sunday condemned lower Broadway and the red light district of Nashville as "the devil's backbone." On that day the crowd included two ladies who happened to be employed in that district, and who rose to leave when they found themselves the subject of the sermon. When Sunday saw this he shouted to the audience, "See, there goes two daughters of the devil." On the way out, one of the ladies turned, waved to Sunday and shouted back, "Good-bye, Daddy!"

Revivals and religious meetings remained an integral part of the Ryman story throughout its history. Early crusades were conducted by N.B. Hardeman, Aimee Semple McPherson and Dwight L. Moody. Guest speakers were as diverse as the great educator Booker T. Washington, who spoke to the General Conference of the Colored Methodist Episcopal Church in 1902, and the evangelist Sister P. Harrell, who was billed as a divine healer, and whose services included the anointing of cripples with oil and the blessing of handkerchiefs for believers.

Heavenly Angel Food Delight

1 angel food cake
1 envelope unflavored gelatin
¼ cup cold water
6 egg yolks, beaten
¾ cup sugar
¾ cup lemon juice
1½ teaspoons grated lemon peel
6 egg whites
¾ cup sugar
1 cup whipping cream
½ cup confectioners' sugar
Cherries and thin lemon slices

Trim the brown edges from the cake and tear the cake into medium-size pieces. Soften the gelatin in the cold water in a double boiler. Add the egg yolks, ¼ cup sugar, lemon juice and lemon peel and mix well. Cook over hot water for 10 minutes, stirring to dissolve the gelatin; cool slightly.

Beat the egg whites with ¾ cup sugar in a mixer bowl until stiff peaks form. Fold into the cooled custard. Layer the cake and the custard ⅓ at a time in a 10-inch tube pan. Chill overnight. Dip into a pan of hot water for 2 seconds and unmold onto a serving plate.

Beat the whipping cream with the confectioners' sugar in a mixer bowl until soft peaks form. Spread over the top and side of the dessert. Garnish with the cherries and lemon slices. Chill until serving time.

Yield: 12 servings.

Homemade Mincemeat Pies

This recipe, from Mrs. Peale, was Reverend Peale's favorite Christmas dessert.

1 pound lean ground beef
8 ounces suet, ground
2½ cups packed brown sugar
1 cup orange juice
¼ cup lemon juice
4½ cups raisins
2½ cups dried currants
½ cup chopped candied fruit
2 pounds tart apples, peeled, sliced
2½ cups water
1½ teaspoons grated orange peel
1 teaspoon grated lemon peel
½ teaspoon cinnamon
½ teaspoon nutmeg
¼ teaspoon mace
Salt to taste
Pastry for 6 (2-crust) pies

Norman Vincent Peale

Combine the ground beef, suet, brown sugar, orange juice, lemon juice, raisins, currants and candied fruit in a large saucepan. Cook over low heat until the brown sugar melts, stirring constantly. Add the apples, water, orange peel, lemon peel, cinnamon, nutmeg, mace and salt and mix well. Simmer until the apples are tender. Spoon 2 cups of the mixture into a pastry-lined pie plate for each pie and top with additional pastry; trim and crimp edges and cut vents.

Bake at 400 degrees for 35 to 40 minutes or until golden brown. May freeze mincemeat in 2-cup portions for later use.

Yield: 6 pies.

Later years brought such religious leaders as Norman Vincent Peale to the Ryman Auditorium. The Ryman meeting was one of the more than one hundred engagements he honored each year until he was ninety-three, to an estimated live audience of twenty million. His message was not to the masses, however, but to the solitary individual who was overwhelmed by life. At the Ryman, he preached his simple formula, which was "picturize, prayerize and actualize solutions."

23

The Fisk Jubilee Singers are credited with introducing the spiritual or jubilee song to the musical world and with saving the university from financial ruin in the process. It is appropriate that these songs, born of religious inspiration gained at church meetings, have figured so prominently in the history of the Ryman, as the Singers have taken part in numerous musical and religious programs held there over the years. In 1941, they joined with renowned black tenor Roland Hayes to offer a concert to benefit Nashville's General Hospital.

The original Fisk University Jubilee Singers

Sponge Cake

This recipe is reprinted exactly as it was contributed by Mrs. William A. Crosthwait to the Fisk Club Cookbook *or* Receipts Contributed by Members of the Club and Friends, *published in the early twentieth century.*

> *6 eggs*
> *2 cups sugar*
> *2 cups flour sifted four times*
> *A little salt*
> *Flavoring to taste*

Beat the yolks light in sugar one at a time. Add the flavoring, then the stiffly beaten whites, and last of all the flour previously sifted.

This is a fine recipe for sponge cake. The reason most people fail with sponge cake is because they beat after the flour is added. This must not be done.

Lemon Angel Roll

1 (1-step) package angel food cake mix
1 (21-ounce) can lemon pie filling
½ cup confectioners' sugar
8 ounces cream cheese, softened
½ cup margarine, softened
4 cups confectioners' sugar
1 teaspoon vanilla extract

Combine the cake mix and pie filling in a mixer bowl and beat until smooth. Spread in an ungreased 10x15-inch cake pan. Bake at 350 degrees for 20 to 25 minutes or until the cake tests done. Invert onto a towel sprinkled with ½ cup confectioners' sugar.

Roll the cake up in the towel and let cool. Beat the cream cheese and margarine in a mixer bowl until light. Add 4 cups confectioners' sugar and vanilla and beat until smooth. Unroll the cake and spread with the cream cheese mixture.

Roll to enclose the filling; place on a serving plate. Drizzle with a confectioners' sugar glaze. Slice to serve.

Yield: 12 servings.

Down the years, a number of choirs besides the Fisk University Jubilee Singers have appreciated the wonderful acoustics of the Ryman and been appreciated by audiences there. The Auditorium resounded to the heavenly voices of the Vatican Choir early in its history and later entertained the Boys Choir of Harlem under the auspices of the Black Children's Institute of Nashville.

FROM GRANDMOTHER'S COOKBOOK

Angel's Food Cake

*Whites of eleven eggs,
One cup of flour,
One and one-half cups of sugar,
One teaspoonful of cream of tartar,
One teaspoonful of almond extract.
Sift flour and sugar together five times, then add cream of tartar.
Have whites well beaten and add sugar and flour slowly,
then almond extract. Beat very little after flour goes in and bake in
round cake pan in moderate oven for about fifty minutes.*

Bavarian Cream

This recipe from the Peay family is from Mrs. Austin Peay's collection.

2 envelopes unflavored gelatin
½ cup cold water
4 egg yolks
1 cup sugar
2 cups light cream or half-and-half, scalded
2 teaspoons vanilla extract
2 cups whipping cream, whipped

Soften the gelatin in the cold water in a bowl. Beat the egg yolks with the sugar in a mixer bowl until thick and light yellow. Combine with the scalded cream in a double boiler. Cook until the mixture thickens, stirring constantly; remove from the heat.

Add the vanilla and gelatin and stir until the gelatin dissolves and the mixture cools. Fold in the whipped cream. Spoon into a mold. Chill until firm. Unmold onto a serving plate.

Yield: 12 servings.

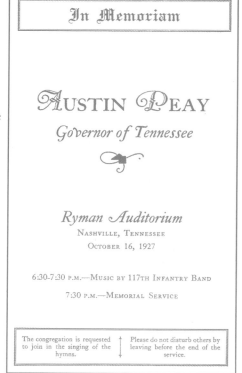

In Memoriam

AUSTIN PEAY
Governor of Tennessee

Ryman Auditorium
NASHVILLE, TENNESSEE
OCTOBER 16, 1927

6:30-7:30 P.M.—MUSIC BY 117TH INFANTRY BAND

7:30 P.M.—MEMORIAL SERVICE

The congregation is requested to join in the singing of the hymns. | Please do not disturb others by leaving before the end of the service.

Churches have always been the setting for funerals and memorial services and the Ryman is no exception. Starting with the funeral of Tom Ryman in 1904, the Auditorium has been the scene of memorial services for various people— from William Jennings Bryan to Roger Miller. The memorial service of Tennessee Governor Austin Peay was conducted there on October 16, 1927, with music by the 117th Infantry Band.

Program courtesy of Nashville Room, Nashville and Davidson County Library

Fudge Cake

Steve Shields' aunt won the grand prize in the chocolate cake division of the 1952 Iowa State Fair with this traditional recipe.

3 cups cake flour
1 teaspoon baking soda
¾ teaspoon salt
¾ cup butter, softened
2¼ cups sugar
1½ teaspoons vanilla extract
3 eggs
3 (1-ounce) squares
    unsweetened chocolate,
    melted
1½ cups ice water

Sculptor Steve Shields with sculpture of Tom Ryman

Sift the cake flour with the baking soda and salt and set aside. Cream the butter, sugar and vanilla in a mixer bowl until fluffy. Add the eggs and chocolate and beat until light. Add the flour mixture alternately with the ice water, mixing well after each addition. Spoon into a 9x13-inch cake pan.

Bake at 350 degrees for 45 to 50 minutes or until the cake tests done. Frost as desired. May bake in three 8-inch cake pans for 30 to 35 minutes if preferred.

Yield: 15 servings.

Steve Shields did the imposing sculpture of Tom Ryman that stands at the new entrance to the restored Ryman. He got the horizontal and vertical dimensions from a photograph, but he had no depth dimensions and was forced to use his own measurements, thinking no one would know. Everyone seemed to agree that he had captured the likeness of Tom Ryman, but a few commented that from the side it looked a bit like Shields. "I knew I had lost that battle when my seven-year-old nephew from Alabama came to visit and said, 'Look, Dad, a sculpture of Uncle Steve.'"

Photograph courtesy of Donnie Beauchamp

Pepper Steak

Faye Speer serves this easy dish to her singing family.

> 1 large round steak
> 2 envelopes onion soup mix
> 2 green bell peppers, cut into strips

Trim the steak and cut into strips. Brown the strips on all sides in a skillet sprayed with nonstick cooking spray. Sprinkle with the onion soup mix and add just enough water to cover.

Cook, covered, until the steak is tender. Add the green peppers. Cook for 5 minutes longer. Serve over rice. May thicken gravy if desired.

Yield: 4 servings.

Gospel singing became a regular part of the Ryman fare with Wally Foster's interdenominational All-Night Gospel Sings, beginning in 1948 and rivaling the Opry in numbers and enthusiasm. Gospel music groups were also a popular part of the Opry program at the Ryman, and the award-winning Singing Speer Family was part of that tradition. The "first family of gospel music" traces its roots to 1921 and is now into the third generation of ministry through song, offering what they call a "middle-of-the-road traditional" approach to Christian music.

The Singing Speer Family

Photograph courtesy of Gospel Music Association Archives

The Cathedrals

Broccoli Salad

This recipe is from Labreeska Hemphill of the singing Hemphill family.

> 4 cups chopped fresh broccoli
> 8 slices bacon, crisp-fried, crumbled
> ½ cup raisins
> ½ cup chopped onion
> ½ cup nuts
> ¾ cup mayonnaise
> ½ cup sugar
> 2 tablespoons vinegar

Combine the broccoli, bacon, raisins, onion and nuts in a salad bowl. Mix the mayonnaise, sugar and vinegar in a small bowl. Add to the salad and toss to mix well. Chill until serving time.

Yield: 8 servings.

Photograph courtesy of Gospel Music Association Archives

Other gospel music groups who brought their message to the Ryman include the Hemphills, the Cathedrals and the LeFevres. The various groups see their music as a ministry of encouragement as well as entertainment, sharing the genuine quality of personal Christianity through songs of faith. For a while, fans also enjoyed the "Grand Ole Opry Gospel Time" at the Ryman, a Sunday afternoon show created by E.W. Wendell to recognize the close links between country and gospel music.

"Sam's Place — Music for the Spirit," the Ryman Auditorium's Sunday night inspirational music series, continues in the vein inaugurated by Sam Jones, for whom it is named. Hosted by award–winning singer/songwriter Gary Chapman since 1994, the music is spiritually based and is performed in an informal setting by artists who share a common faith. Of the Ryman, Gary Chapman says that "I am honored to work and play there and call it my home. More importantly, I call the people I work with there my friends. The decades of those kinds of relationships echo off the walls of that glorious old building and resound in a special place in my heart."

Italian Cream Cake with Frosting

Gary Chapman shares this favorite cake recipe with us.

½ cup margarine, softened
½ cup shortening
2 cups sugar
5 egg yolks
2 cups sifted flour
1 teaspoon baking soda
Salt to taste
1 cup buttermilk
8 ounces coconut
5 egg whites, stiffly beaten
8 ounces cream cheese, softened
½ cup margarine, softened
1 (1-pound) package confectioners' sugar
1 teaspoon vanilla extract
½ cup chopped pecans

Gary Chapman and friends at "Sam's Place"

Cream ½ cup margarine, shortening and sugar in a mixer bowl until light and fluffy. Beat in the egg yolks. Add the flour, baking soda, salt and buttermilk and mix well. Stir in the coconut. Fold in the egg whites. Spoon into 3 greased and floured cake pans.

Bake at 350 degrees for 30 minutes. Cool in the pans for several minutes. Remove to a wire rack to cool completely. Beat the cream cheese and ½ cup margarine in a mixer bowl until light. Add the confectioners' sugar and vanilla and mix until smooth. Stir in the pecans. Spread between the layers and over the top and side of the cake.

Yield: 16 servings.

Photograph courtesy of Donnie Beauchamp

Buttermilk Fudge

Amy is grateful to her Grandmother Grant for this fudge recipe.

    2 cups sugar
    1 cup buttermilk
    1 teaspoon baking soda
    2 tablespoons butter
    1 teaspoon vanilla extract
    1 cup chopped nuts

Mix the sugar, buttermilk and baking soda in a saucepan. Cook over medium heat until the sugar dissolves, stirring constantly. Cook to 234 to 240 degrees on a candy thermometer, soft-ball stage; remove from the heat. Stir in the butter and vanilla. Beat until the mixture thickens and loses its gloss. Stir in the nuts. Pour onto a buttered platter and let stand until firm. Cut into squares.

Yield: 2 pounds.

Gary Chapman with Amy Grant

Photograph courtesy of Donnie Beauchamp

Amy Grant has appeared on "Sam's Place" at the Ryman and has fond memories of going to the Ryman as a child. "One of my strongest recollections, as a preadolescent sitting in the balcony, was the entrance of a young Dolly Parton onto that stage. I was immediately filled with great anticipation at the prospects of womanhood."

"Sam's Place" has featured the finest entertainers in pop, contemporary Christian, bluegrass, country and gospel music, including Steven Curtis Chapman, Alison Krauss, dc Talk, and CeCe Winans, to name a few. While it prides itself on the diversity of the artists who perform, "Sam's Place" underscores a common theme: Music for the Spirit.

Chicken Hawaiian

Steven Curtis Chapman likes this easy way to marinate and grill chicken.

2 cups pineapple juice
½ cup packed brown sugar
1 cup catsup
¼ cup Worcestershire sauce
2 cloves of garlic, minced
8 chicken breast halves, skinned, boned

Combine the pineapple juice, brown sugar, catsup, Worcestershire sauce and garlic in a shallow dish and stir to dissolve the brown sugar. Rinse the chicken and pat dry. Add to the marinade, coating well. Marinate, covered, in the refrigerator for 8 hours or longer. Drain, reserving the marinade.

Sear the chicken on both sides over hot coals. Reduce the grill temperature. Grill over low coals until the chicken is cooked through. Heat the reserved marinade in a small saucepan. Serve with the chicken as dipping sauce.

Yield: 8 servings.

Steven Curtis Chapman with Gary Chapman and Alison Krauss at "Sam's Place"

Photograph courtesy of Donnie Beauchamp

Australian Meat Pie

The Newsboys offer this recipe from their native Australia.

The Newsboys

1½ pounds steak, minced
1 onion, chopped
1½ cups beef stock
½ cup tomato sauce
Nutmeg, salt and pepper
  to taste
2 tablespoons flour
1 unbaked (9-inch)
  deep-dish pie shell
1 sheet frozen puff
  pastry, thawed
1 egg, beaten

Brown the steak with the onion in a skillet, stirring constantly; drain. Add the beef stock, tomato sauce, nutmeg, salt and pepper and mix well. Simmer, covered, for 15 minutes. Blend the flour with enough water to make a thin paste. Stir into the skillet. Cook until thickened, stirring constantly. Cool to room temperature. Spoon into the pie shell. Top with the puff pastry, pressing down gently to seal the edges; trim the edges and cut vents. Brush with the egg.

Bake at 450 degrees for 10 minutes. Reduce the oven temperature to 350 degrees. Bake for 10 minutes longer or until golden brown.

Yield: 4 to 6 servings.

The Newsboys are six award-winning manic Australian personalities with an up-front faith message who bill themselves as a contemporary Christian music rock band. They brought their compelling stage presence to the Ryman for the first Nashville Area Music Awards. Their message can be summed up in one of their songs, "Reality:" "the world heads off in its own direction, doing what's right in its own eyes, thinking it's living reality. But the real true reality, God's reality, will welcome us back."

Michael W. Smith's favorite memory of singing at the Ryman was in the fall of 1995. "I was a guest of Gary Chapman's 'Sam's Place' and... As I sat at the piano and began singing 'Angels Unaware' I knew someone very special to me was waiting to join me on stage. On my last phrase, 'maybe we are entertaining angels unaware,' the audience and I held our breath as my beautiful nine-year-old daughter walked on stage, a vision in white. My own little angel joined me and finished the song. I don't think there was a dry eye in the place. I'll never forget it."

Vegetable Burritos

Debbie Smith says that these are favorites with the Smith children.

½ cup sliced onion
2 tablespoons vegetable oil
1 cup chopped drained artichoke hearts
1 cup chopped fresh or frozen spinach, drained
1¼ cups chopped tomatoes
1 (4-ounce) can chopped green chiles
½ teaspoon oregano
¼ teaspoon each basil, cumin and pepper
1 cup shredded Monterey Jack cheese
12 (8-inch) flour tortillas

Sauté the onion in the oil in a skillet for 2 to 3 minutes. Add the artichoke hearts, spinach, tomatoes, green chiles, seasonings and half the cheese and mix well. Spoon onto the tortillas and roll to enclose the filling. Arrange in a greased baking dish.

Bake, covered with foil, at 350 degrees for 15 minutes. Sprinkle with the remaining cheese. Bake, uncovered, for 5 minutes longer. Top with salsa, sour cream and guacamole.

Yield: 6 servings.

Whitney Smith

Photograph courtesy of Jessica Atteberry

34

Grilled Chicken Tostadas

The flavor of the West that the Riders in the Sky brings to audiences is reflected in their enjoyment of the flavors of Southwest cooking.

4 boneless skinless chicken breasts
1 teaspoon ground cumin
¼ cup fresh orange juice
¼ cup salsa
1 tablespoon vegetable oil
2 cloves of garlic, minced
1 (16-ounce) can refried beans
2 tablespoons salsa
4 (10-inch) flour tortillas
1 head Romaine lettuce, shredded
1½ cups shredded Monterey Jack cheese with jalapeños
1 avocado, chopped
1 tomato, seeded, chopped

Riders in the Sky Woody Paul, Ranger Doug, and Too Slim

Rinse the chicken and pat dry. Place in a shallow dish and sprinkle with the cumin. Pour a mixture of the orange juice, ¼ cup salsa, oil and garlic over the chicken. Marinate, covered, in the refrigerator for 2 to 8 hours, turning occasionally. Combine the beans and 2 tablespoons salsa in a small saucepan. Simmer until heated through, stirring occasionally; keep hot. Drain the chicken, reserving the marinade. Grill, covered, over medium coals for 10 minutes, brushing on both sides with the reserved marinade. Place the tortillas in a single layer on the grill and pierce with the tip of a knife to prevent puffing. Grill for 1 to 2 minutes on each side or until golden brown. Slice the chicken crosswise into ½-inch strips. Place the tortillas on serving plates. Spread with the bean mixture. Top with the lettuce, chicken, cheese, avocado and tomato. Garnish with sour cream and chopped cilantro.

Yield: 4 servings.

Woody Paul, Ranger Doug and Too Slim of the Riders in the Sky joined Ricky Skaggs and Bill Monroe to sing hymns at the Ryman Centennial Celebration. Appearing at the Ryman is like coming home for Woody, who says that he grew up as part of the woodwork backstage at the Ryman growing up. "Sam and Kirk McGee took me under their wing and I was just always there. I would have never gone to college if Roy Acuff and Howdy Forester hadn't kicked my behind to do so. They were wonderful guys. That dressing room door was never closed. When I look back on those days, I realize Acuff was a pretty selfless guy to do that. So I went to Vanderbilt and then to MIT, and I guess you could say I did what they told me to do. And then I came back to play fiddle."

35

The Mother Church has also enjoyed her share of happy sacraments and counts several weddings among the ceremonies celebrated there. Pete and Euneta Kirby were married at the Ryman on May 15, 1993. As Brother Oswald of the Grand Ole Opry, Pete has many happy memories of playing there himself, but the music on this occasion was provided by Roy Acuff, who sang "Tied Down," and Bill Carlisle, who sang "Too Old To Cut the Mustard"; additional music was provided by Charlie Collins, Howdy Forester, Sally Forester and the Foresters' son Bobby.

Chocolate Pie

Chocolate must be the way to a man's heart, because this is the pie that Euneta served to Brother Oswald when they were dating.

1 cup sugar
4 to 6 tablespoons cornstarch
¼ cup baking cocoa
½ teaspoon salt
2 to 3 egg yolks
2 cups milk
2 tablespoons butter or margarine
1 teaspoon vanilla extract
1 baked (8- or 9-inch) pie shell
2 egg whites

The wedding of Pete (Brother Oswald) and Euneta Kirby at the Ryman

Mix ¾ cup of the sugar, cornstarch, baking cocoa and salt in a saucepan. Add the eggs yolks and milk and mix well. Cook over low to medium heat until thickened, stirring constantly; remove from the heat. Add the butter and vanilla. Spoon into the pie shell.

Beat the egg whites until soft peaks form. Add ¼ cup sugar and beat until stiff peaks form. Spread over the pie, sealing to the edge. Bake at 300 degrees just until golden brown.

Yield: 6 to 8 servings.

Raisin Bread

Trisha bakes this bread in three one-pound cans. The recipe came from one of her favorite teachers, Margaret McElheney.

Trisha Yearwood and Robert
Reynolds at their Ryman wedding

1 cup boiling water
1½ cups raisins
2 teaspoons baking soda
1½ cups flour
1 cup crushed bran cereal
1 cup sugar
¼ teaspoon salt
1 egg
¼ cup vegetable oil

Pour the boiling water over the raisins and baking soda in a bowl and mix well. Let stand until cool. Mix the flour, bran cereal, sugar and salt in a large bowl. Beat the egg lightly with the oil in a small bowl. Add to the flour mixture and mix well. Stir in the raisin mixture. Spoon into 3 greased 1-pound cans.

Bake at 350 degrees for 45 minutes. Cool in the cans for several minutes, then invert onto a wire rack to cool completely.

Yield: 3 loaves.

May 21, 1994, was the date of Trisha Yearwood's marriage to Robert Reynolds of the Mavericks at the Ryman (see Preface by Will Campbell). Trisha says that "The Ryman was a church before it was the Mother Church of Country Music, so we thought it was a perfect place to blend the spiritual side with the music." The newly refurbished Auditorium was decorated with sunflowers for the storybook event, and the bridesmaids carried sunflowers and wore black western dresses. The groom and groomsmen wore traditional tailcoats. The bride wore a trim formal pantsuit and walked down the aisle to "The Tennessee Waltz" played by Del McCoury's band.

MUSIC
HALL

...HITTING THE HIGH NOTES

The Ryman was built at the exact same time as another famous auditorium — New York's Carnegie Hall. Although that hall has become synonymous with the fine arts and the world's most famous performers, the Ryman's roster reveals its share of culture, too.

Like many things, the broadening of the Ryman's horizons from a house of primarily religious and moral righteousness to a hall for entertainment came out of the need for cash. In the late 1890s, the trustees had a big debt to deal with and the appetite for other forms of entertainment among Nashvillians — many of whom had given generously to the Ryman's construction — was increasing. Although some non-religious events had taken place there from the beginning, opening the Ryman to even wider use was the only thing to do. Even Tom Ryman, who was still involved at the time, agreed.

Thus began the Ryman's decades of remarkable and widely diverse bookings, although it always remained a favorite for religious conventions and church groups.

The Ryman's international flavor flourished in its first twenty years, as classical music's most famous artists lined up for their turn on its stage. The auditorium's love affair with bands and symphonies — or vice versa — began as early as the late 1800s when the Theodore Thomas Orchestra played the unfinished Tabernacle. Thomas was the founder of the Chicago Symphony.

Shortly thereafter John Philip Sousa and his famous U.S. Marine Corps Band played here, and the best big-band sounds — like Wayne King, Spike Jones, and Fred Waring — resounded from the Ryman during their heyday.

Great symphonies from New York, Philadelphia, and abroad came to play. Russian composer Rachmaninoff stormed through his dark compositions here, and many of the world's virtuoso musicians took their turn on the Ryman stage. The hall's fabulous acoustics became renowned, and performers were eager to experience them.

The Ryman continued to thrive, even during the Great Depression, thanks largely to the efforts of Lula Naff. Naff was a secretary and book-

"If they'd just give me the Ryman back with its dust and paint and a big block of tickets, I wouldn't ask anything else."

—Lula Naff, after her retirement

Lula Naff (right) with the Auditorium Improvement Board in 1948
Photograph courtesy of F. Robinson Collection, Vanderbilt University Library

*I am honored to work
and play there and call
it my home. More
importantly, I call the
people I work with there
my friends. The
decades of those kinds of
relationships echo off
the walls of that glorious
old building and
resound in a special
place in my heart.*
—*Gary Chapman*

keeper for one of the groups that early on booked entertainment in the Ryman. When the group dissolved, Naff began to book the Ryman herself. She proved so capable, the board of trustees in effect made her general manager in 1920. She remained at the Ryman until her retirement in 1955.

It was Naff who brought some of the greatest names in music to the Ryman's stage. Her keen business instincts told her that famous names would sell tickets, and she proved right. Through the years, Nelson Eddy, Jeanette MacDonald, Victor Borge, Pete Fountain, Doris Day, and Dinah Shore would all perform here. Later, Emmylou Harris and Neil Diamond would sing. Even Roy Rogers and Dale Evans — with Trigger — crooned a tune from this stage, and the Nashville Symphony called it home for a period of time.

When television came to the Ryman in the fifties, it broadened the musical horizons even more. The country and bluegrass traditions, now well established here, continued on an ABC show called "Stars of the Grand Ole Opry," starring Minnie Pearl, Rod Brasfield, and Roy Acuff. Some time later, Opry sponsor Martha White Flour did a Christmas special from the Ryman.

That was just the beginning of many television shows originating from the Ryman. During the next 20 years, Arlene Francis, Barbara Mandrell, Dolly Parton, Jimmy Dean, and Porter Wagoner would broadcast all or part of their shows from the Ryman. Elvis Presley even appeared as part of an Opry program in 1954. In 1969, "The Johnny Cash Show" began airing from the Ryman, bringing a whole new genre of music to the old stage. While we may view them now as soft rockers or even folk singers, at the time people like Neil Young, James Taylor, and Linda Ronstadt were cutting edge. Those who were lucky enough to be a part of the live audience for those tapings cherish the memories.

Sauerbraten

This recipe celebrates the performance by the Theodore Thomas Orchestra, which, with numbers from Wagner performed by Ida Klein, soprano, and Hans Von-Schiller, pianist, had a decidedly Germanic flavor. Serve it with potato pancakes and red cabbage for a real German treat.

2 medium onions, sliced
1 carrot, sliced
1 rib celery, sliced
2 cups red wine vinegar
1 sprig of parsley
1 teaspoon thyme
1 tablespoon pickling spice
1 tablespoon salt
1 (4- to 5-pound) bottom round roast
2 tablespoons butter
2 tablespoons olive oil
Salt and pepper to taste
4 to 5 tablespoons cornstarch
¼ cup water

THEODORE THOMAS.

Combine the onions, carrot, celery, vinegar, parsley, thyme, pickling spice and 1 tablespoon salt in a large bowl and mix well. Add the beef. Marinate, covered, in the refrigerator for 3 days or longer, turning the beef once a day. Drain, reserving the marinade. Brown the beef on all sides in a mixture of the butter and olive oil in a heavy saucepan. Strain the reserved marinade into the saucepan. Simmer for 3 to 4 hours or until tender.

Remove the roast to a serving plate. Bring the pan drippings to a boil and season with salt and pepper to taste. Stir in a mixture the cornstarch and water gradually. Cook until thickened, stirring constantly. Serve with the roast.

Yield: 8 to 10 servings.

Realization dawned early that the Tabernacle, in order to pay its bills, would have to host secular as well as religious events, and music quickly assumed a continuing role in its history. One of the largest early performances was in 1892 in the nearly finished Tabernacle by the orchestra led by Theodore Thomas, founder and conductor of the Chicago Symphony Orchestra. The gate was, sadly, insufficient to pay Mr. Thomas' expenses and added nothing to the depleted building fund. Eventually the debt to him was canceled.

Sweet Potatoes and Apples

After Uncle Jimmy fiddled the bugs off the sweet 'tater vine, he might have enjoyed this dish prepared with the 'taters.

6 large red baking apples
½ cup packed light brown
    sugar
5 cups mashed cooked sweet
    potatoes
6 tablespoons butter
6 tablespoons whipping cream
½ teaspoon cinnamon
½ cup packed light
    brown sugar
2 tablespoons melted butter

Uncle Jimmy Thompson and George D. Hay with his steamboat whistle "Hushpuckena"

Cut the apples into halves lengthwise and discard the cores. Arrange in a shallow baking dish. Sprinkle with ½ cup brown sugar and add a small amount of water.

Bake at 400 degrees for 10 to 20 minutes or until slightly tender. Scoop out the pulp and reserve the pulp and ½-inch shells. Combine the apple pulp with the sweet potatoes, 6 tablespoons butter, whipping cream and cinnamon in a bowl and beat until smooth.

Spoon into the apple shells and arrange in a shallow baking dish. Sprinkle with ½ cup brown sugar and drizzle with the melted butter. Bake for 20 minutes or until heated through.

Yield: 12 servings.

Photograph courtesy of Grand Ole Opry Archives

Corn Pones

This recipe is from Mary Littell Rust Ellis, daughter of Littell Rust. Littell was Naff's head usher when he was eighteen and went on to become her lifelong attorney, advisor and friend. Mrs. Ellis tells us that Mrs. Naff was never known to have cooked and may have been the original "take out" customer.

> *2 cups cornmeal*
> *½ teaspoon baking soda*
> *½ to 1 teaspoon salt*
> *1 cup (scant) buttermilk*
> *3 tablespoons melted shortening*

Mix the cornmeal, baking soda and salt in a bowl. Add the buttermilk and shortening and mix well. Shape with damp hands into pones. Place on a heated greased griddle or skillet.

Bake at 400 degrees for 15 minutes or until golden brown.

Yield: 6 servings.

Much of the success of the Ryman Auditorium was due to the efforts of Lula Naff, general manager from 1920 until 1955. She realized that the Ryman would have to present a popular mix of entertainment in order to pay its bills. A shrewd businesswoman and colorful character in her own right, she liked to be addressed by the businesslike name "L.C. Naff." She was reputed to have always dressed in black and to have carried the Ryman's tickets and money in a shirt box, sometimes just stuffing them in her purse and paying no attention to the fact that it was so full it wouldn't close.

Lula C. Naff, colorful and successful manager of the Ryman for over thirty years

Photograph courtesy of F. Robinson Collection, Vanderbilt University Library

A famous story of the Ryman
involves Lula Naff's engagement of the famous Irish tenor
John McCormack in 1916 for
his only southern stop. In
a coy public relations move,
Naff did not deny rumors
that she had taken a second
mortgage on her house to
underwrite the performance.
With that publicity she sold
5,000 tickets for 4,000 seats,
and three hundred people
ended up sitting on the stage,
where they couldn't hear well.
McCormack finally turned
his back on the auditorium for
one song to appease the
unfortunate stage-sitters.

Boxty-on-the-Pan

This traditional Irish dish must have very familiar to John McCormack, who held the honor of drawing more people to the Ryman in Naff's day than any other artist.

> 1 cup grated raw potato
> 1 cup flour
> 2 teaspoons baking powder
> 2 teaspoons salt
> 1 cup mashed cooked potato
> 2 eggs, beaten
> ¼ cup (about) milk
> Melted butter

Squeeze the grated potato in a cheesecloth to remove as much moisture as possible. Sift the flour, baking powder and salt into a bowl. Add the grated potato, mashed potato, eggs and enough milk to make a batter that can be dropped from a spoon. Drop by tablespoonfuls into melted butter in a heated skillet. Cook over medium heat for 4 minutes on each side or until golden brown. Serve hot with butter and sugar if desired.

Yield: 6 servings.

FROM GRANDMOTHER'S COOKBOOK

Boxty-on-the-Griddle

My mother took a couple of grated raw potatoes and a skillet of hot mashed potatoes, 3 or 4 handfuls of flour with a bit of butter rubbed in and a generous grain of salt — all mixed well and rolled out on the board, cut into squares, and baked on a greased griddle to the tune of the children singing, "Three pans of boxty, baking all the day. What use is boxty without a cup of tay?"

Frozen Fruit Salad

1 large can fruit salad
1 cup mayonnaise
1/2 pint whipping cream
Whip cream very stiff, mix with mayonnaise, then add fruit to mixture.
Nuts may be added if desired. Pour mixture in trays and place in
Williams Ice-O-Matic Refrigerator to freeze. Serve in shredded lettuce
with a bit of whipped cream and mayonnaise on salad.

Frozen Cranberry Salad

*It was probably not cold enough in Helen Morgan's dressing room in 1936
to freeze this salad.*

1 cup whipping cream
8 ounces cream cheese, softened
2 cups confectioners' sugar
1 cup mayonnaise
1 cup chopped pecans
2 (16-ounce) cans whole cranberry sauce

Whip the cream in a mixer bowl until soft peaks form. Add the cream
cheese, confectioners' sugar, mayonnaise and pecans and mix well.

Spread the cranberry sauce evenly in a 9x13-inch dish. Spread the
cream mixture over the top. Freeze until firm. Let stand at room
temperature for 5 minutes before serving. Cut into squares and serve
on lettuce-lined plates.

Yield: 15 servings.

Not all singers engaged by Lula
Naff to sing at the Ryman were
pleased with the experience.
Soprano Frances Alda, appearing
in support of World War I
veterans in 1919, was furious
that ticket sales were slim and
threatened not to sing. News
that her pique would be aired in
the newspapers convinced her
to perform, but she dashed out
without giving an encore.
Helen Morgan was incensed
because her dressing room
was cold, a perennial problem
at the Ryman in the early days.
She sent her manager out after
business hours looking for
an electric heater, which he found
in time to warm up the sultry
voice of the torch singer.

John Philip Sousa

John Philip Sousa was a popular early performer at the Ryman. He took the rather simple form of the military march and gave it a personal style and new rhythmic and melodic vitality that audiences at the Ryman loved. His rousing renditions of the marches he wrote for the marine and navy bands were in particular demand on his world tours just before and after World War I.

"Stars and Stripes Forever" Salad

This salad echoes the motif of the more than 100 patriotic marches that John Philip Sousa wrote. Its red, white and blue colors make it a perfect addition to a Fourth of July picnic.

> 1 (10-ounce) package frozen raspberries, thawed
> 2 (3-ounce) packages raspberry gelatin
> 2 cups boiling water
> 1 pint raspberry sherbet
> 1 (6-ounce) can frozen lemonade concentrate, thawed
> Blueberries
> Sour cream

Drain the raspberries, reserving the syrup. Dissolve the gelatin in the boiling water in a bowl. Add the sherbet 1 spoonful at a time, mixing well until melted. Stir in the lemonade concentrate and reserved raspberry syrup. Fold in the raspberries. Spoon into a ring mold.

Chill until firm. Unmold onto a serving plate. Fill the center with blueberries. Top with sour cream.

Yield: 8 servings.

Photograph courtesy of Nashville Room, Nashville and Davidson County Library

Jazzy Crab-Stuffed Mushrooms

Appetizers probably enjoyed a growing popularity in the jazzy 1920s of speakeasies and cocktails.

1 pound fresh mushrooms
6 ounces crab meat, drained
¼ cup finely chopped celery
¼ cup finely chopped green onions
¼ cup mayonnaise
½ cup cracker crumbs
4 ounces Parmesan cheese, grated

Wipe the mushrooms, discarding the stems. Combine the crab meat, celery, green onions, mayonnaise and cracker crumbs in a bowl and mix well. Stir in half the cheese. Spoon the mixture into the mushroom caps and arrange in a 9x13-inch baking dish. Sprinkle with the remaining cheese.

Bake at 350 degrees for 10 to 15 minutes or until the cheese melts. Serve immediately.

Yield: 12 servings.

Paul Whiteman brought his "experiment in American music" to the Ryman in the 1920s, defying earlier tastes and subduing without devitalizing that wild American creature known as jazz. Critics claimed that by using scores and arrangements, in addition to employing a band that consisted of soloists of note, Whiteman moved jazz "out of the kitchen and upstairs to the parlor."

Art courtesy of F. Robinson Collection, Vanderbilt University Library

The Don Cossack Russian Male Chorus, known as the Singing Horsemen of the Steppes, had an enthusiastic reception when they appeared at the Ryman in 1931. The unaccompanied group, using choral effects that imitated instruments and distant bells, offered rousing renditions of the "Volga Boat Song" and Bortniansky's "Who Can Equal Thee."

Russian Meat Cakes

The Cossacks would have been familiar with this dish, introduced to the steppes of Russia by the Mongols in the thirteenth century. The cakes can also be made with egg in the pastry and can be simmered instead of deep-fried. They would have been served with butter and sour cream and small glasses of vodka.

2 pounds lean ground beef
4 ounces finely ground pork
1 cup finely chopped onion
1 cup warm water
Salt and pepper to taste
4 cups wheat flour
1 teaspoon salt
1 cup milk
1 cup (about) water
Vegetable oil for deep-frying

Brown the ground beef and pork with the onion in a skillet, stirring until the meat is crumbly; drain. Stir in the warm water and salt and pepper to taste. Cook until heated through. Mix the flour and 1 teaspoon salt in a bowl. Add the milk and enough water to form a soft dough. Let rest, covered, for 10 to 15 minutes. Roll on a floured surface and cut into 3- to 4-inch squares. Place 1¼ tablespoons of the filling on each square. Fold the dough over to enclose the filling, sealing the edges. Deep-fry in 375-degree oil until golden brown.

Yield: 8 servings.

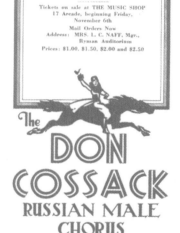

The SINGING HORSEMEN
of the STEPPES

RYMAN AUDITORIUM
Monday Eve., Nov. 9th, 1931
at 8:15 P.M.

Tickets on sale at THE MUSIC SHOP
17 Arcade, beginning Friday,
November 6th
Mail Orders Now
Address: MRS. L. C. NAFF, Mgr.,
Ryman Auditorium
Prices: $1.00, $1.50, $2.00 and $2.50

The DON COSSACK RUSSIAN MALE CHORUS
SERGE JAROFF, Conductor

Management
METROPOLITAN MUSICAL BUREAU
Division of
COLUMBIA CONCERTS CORPORATION
of COLUMBIA BROADCASTING SYSTEM
113 WEST 57th ST.   NEW YORK CITY

Poster courtesy of Nashville Room, Nashville and Davidson County Library

Canadian Meat Pies

This recipe, recalling the Canadian setting of Jeannette McDonald's and Nelson Eddy's famous movie "Rose Marie," is traditionally served after midnight Mass on Christmas Eve.

4½ cups sifted flour
3 teaspoons salt
2 cups shortening
⅔ cup cold water
2 pounds lean ground pork
2 pounds lean ground beef
1 onion, chopped
3 medium potatoes, chopped
½ teaspoon pepper
2 cups water
¼ teaspoon each nutmeg, cinnamon and cloves
Unsalted cracker crumbs
2 tablespoons milk

Jeannette McDonald

Sift the flour and 2 teaspoons of the salt into a bowl. Reserve ¼ cup of the mixture. Cut the shortening into the remaining flour mixture until crumbly. Blend the reserved flour mixture with ⅔ cup cold water. Add to the crumb mixture and mix to form a dough. Chill for 30 minutes. Divide the pastry into 4 portions. Roll 2 of the portions on a floured surface and fit into two 9-inch pie plates. Roll the remaining pastry for the top crusts. Combine the pork, beef, onion, potatoes, the remaining salt, pepper and 2 cups water in a saucepan. Cook for 30 to 45 minutes or until the vegetables are tender, stirring frequently; drain. Mash well. Add the spices and enough cracker crumbs to thicken to the desired consistency. Spoon into the pastry-lined pie plates; top with the remaining pastry. Seal the edges and cut vents. Brush with the milk. Bake at 425 degrees for 45 minutes or until golden brown.

Yield: 12 servings.

Many great singers won the hearts of Ryman audiences, including the tenor Paul Ryman, son of Thomas Ryman, who performed there in 1919. Other popular singers included Emma Eames, Mary Garden, Alessandro Bonci, Marian Anderson, Lily Pons and Alma Gluck. Some, such as Nelson Eddy and Jeannette McDonald, won recognition as a result of appearances in a new entertainment phenomenon: the movies. It was reported that at McDonald's performance at the Ryman, in November of 1940, she was required to give encore after encore.

The famous Polish patriot,

pianist, composer and statesman

Ignace Jan Paderewski

made the first of several visits

to the Ryman in 1908. Naff

claimed that he was the only

pianist that made a profit for the

Auditorium and credited it to

higher seat prices. He gave most

of the money he earned on

concert tours to help his native

Poland. The audiences loved him

and demanded more, but he is

reputed to have taken exception to

the rudeness of hasty patrons

departing to their carriages during

one of the encores. He walked

off the stage, but was persuaded

to return by general applause.

Paderewski's student and fellow

countryman, Arthur Rubenstein,

also performed at the Ryman.

Stuffed Cabbage

Golabki Z Kapusty is one of the most popular dishes in Paderewski's native Poland.

1 large head cabbage
2 slices dried bread
½ cup each chopped green bell pepper and celery
1 small onion, minced
2 tablespoons butter
1 pound ground beef
1 egg
1¼ teaspoons salt
½ teaspoon pepper
1 cup (or more) beef bouillon
3 tablespoons flour
3 tablespoons melted butter
3 tablespoons tomato paste

Ignace Jan Paderewski

Parboil the cabbage in water to cover in a saucepan until the outer leaves separate. Remove 12 large leaves, reserving the remaining cabbage for another use. Trim the tough middle ribs. Soak the bread in enough water to moisten in a bowl. Sauté the green pepper, celery and onion in the butter in a skillet. Add to the bread with the ground beef, egg, salt and pepper and mix well. Spoon onto the cabbage leaves and roll to enclose, tucking in the edges. Arrange close together in a saucepan. Add the bouillon. Simmer until cooked through. Remove to a serving platter, reserving the cooking liquid. Stir the flour into the melted butter in a saucepan. Cook until golden brown, stirring constantly. Stir in the tomato paste and the reserved liquid. Cook until thickened, stirring constantly. Spoon over the cabbage rolls.

Yield: 6 servings.

Alexander Torte

This pastry was named for Czar Alexander of Russia, of the ruling family to which Rachmaninoff gave his allegiance and for whose sake he fled the country in 1917.

  1 cup unsalted butter, chilled
  3 tablespoons sugar
  3 cups flour
  1 egg
  2½ cups confectioners' sugar
  2 teaspoons lemon juice
  ¼ cup (or less) cold water
  ½ to 1 cup raspberry jam

Combine the butter, sugar and flour in a large bowl and mix until crumbly. Add the egg and mix to form a dough. Chill, wrapped in plastic wrap, for 1 hour. Divide the pastry into 2 portions and roll each portion into a circle on a floured surface. Place on a generously buttered and floured baking sheet.

Bake at 250 degrees for 40 minutes or until golden brown. Mix the confectioners' sugar, lemon juice and cold water in a bowl until smooth. Place 1 pastry on a serving plate. Spread with the jam and top with the remaining pastry. Drizzle with the glaze.

Yield: 8 servings.

Sergei Rachmaninoff

Pianists and composers continued to attract enthusiastic crowds to the Ryman, including Vladimir de Pachman, Yehudi Menuhin, and Sergei Rachmaninoff, who voiced their enthusiasm for the Auditorium's acoustics. After fleeing his native Russia during the revolution of 1917, Rachmaninoff became an American citizen and balanced his time between composing and performing, thrilling Ryman audiences with the fire and strength of his playing.

The musical classics were regular offerings at the Ryman, and great conductors brought their symphonies: Walter Damrosch and the New York Symphony Orchestra, Modest Altschuler and the Russian Symphony Orchestra, Eugene Ormandy and the Philadelphia Symphony Orchestra, and Nashville's own Symphony Orchestra.

Soul Pasta

Kenneth Schermerhorn, conductor of the Nashville Symphony, shares this favorite recipe with us.

> 3 pounds young tender mixed kale, turnip and mustard greens
> 3 cups dry white wine
> 10 cloves of garlic, crushed
> 3 tablespoons olive oil
> Steak sauce to taste
> Italian seasoning, salt and pepper to taste
> 16 ounces angel hair pasta, cooked al dente
> Olive oil and grappa to taste
> Grated Parmesan cheese to taste

Remove the large stems from the greens and wash well. Combine with the wine, garlic, 3 tablespoons olive oil, steak sauce, Italian seasoning, salt, pepper and water to just cover in a saucepan. Cook just until tender. Cut into fine strips with scissors.

Combine with the pasta and a small amount of olive oil and grappa in a serving bowl and toss to mix well. Add cheese and toss lightly. Serve immediately.

Yield: 4 servings.

Kenneth Schermerhorn

Pound Cake

Suzanne Potter, who plays with the Nashville Symphony, shared her version of her grandmother's pound cake. She says not to substitute other shortening for the butter in this recipe.

> 1½ cups butter, softened
> 8 ounces cream cheese, softened
> 3 cups sugar
> 6 large eggs, at room temperature
> 3 cups flour
> Salt to taste
> 2 teaspoons vanilla extract
> 1½ teaspoons almond extract

Beat the butter, cream cheese and sugar in a mixer bowl until light and fluffy. Beat in the eggs 1 at a time. Add the flour ½ cup at a time alternately with the salt and flavorings, mixing well after each addition. Spoon into a tube pan.

Bake at 350 degrees for 1½ hours; do not open the oven during the baking time. Cool in the pan for several minutes. Remove to a wire rack to cool completely.

Yield: 16 servings.

Although the Nashville Symphony has a new performing home, it continues to perform occasionally at the Ryman for serious dates as well as for Pops Concerts and Casual Classics. One reason might be that symphony members always look forward to dates at the Ryman because, according to violinist Suzanne Potter, "The sound in the hall is so wonderful. As a performer you can hear yourself play so well and have a sense of relationship with the other musicians."

FROM GRANDMOTHER'S COOKBOOK

Pound Cake

One pound of butter, the same of sugar, same of flour, ten eggs, third of a small nutmeg grated, and the grated peel of half a lemon. Stir the butter and sugar to a cream, add the yolks of the eggs beaten light, then beat the whites to a stiff froth and add them alternately with the flour, flavor, put in a deep round pan and bake in a moderate oven. Try with a broom splint.

Marshmallow World Bars

Ray Anthony might have enjoyed a plate of these with a cup of coffee during his recording session of "Marshmallow World" at the Ryman.

½ cup butter, softened
1 cup sugar
1 teaspoon vanilla extract
2 eggs
¾ cup flour
1 teaspoon baking powder
½ teaspoon salt
1 cup chopped pecans
3 cups miniature marshmallows
6 tablespoons butter
1½ cups confectioners' sugar
1 teaspoon vanilla extract
Hot coffee

Cream ½ cup butter, sugar and 1 teaspoon vanilla in a mixer bowl until light and fluffy. Beat in the eggs. Add the flour, baking powder and salt and mix well. Stir in the pecans. Press into a greased 9x13-inch baking pan. Bake at 350 degrees for 20 minutes. Sprinkle with the marshmallows.

Bake just until the marshmallows are golden brown. Cool on a wire rack. Brown 6 tablespoons butter in a saucepan. Add the confectioners' sugar and 1 teaspoon vanilla and mix well. Add enough coffee to make of spreading consistency. Spread over the baked layer. Cut into bars.

Yield: 3 dozen.

Squash Casserole

This recipe was served to Dinah Shore by Brenda and David Hall, who entertained her during her taping at the Ryman.

> 2 pounds yellow squash, cut into ½- to ¾-inch cubes
> 1 medium onion, coarsely chopped
> 2 cloves of garlic
> Salt and pepper to taste
> 3 tablespoons butter or margarine
> 1 cup cracker crumbs
> ½ cup milk
> 1 egg
> ½ teaspoon salt
> 1 cup shredded Cheddar cheese

Cook the squash with the onion and garlic in boiling salted and peppered water to cover in a saucepan for 10 minutes or just until tender. Drain, discarding the garlic. Combine the vegetables with the butter, cracker crumbs, milk, egg, ½ teaspoon salt, pepper to taste and half the cheese in a bowl and mix well. Spoon into a buttered baking dish and sprinkle with the remaining cheese. Bake at 350 degrees for 20 to 30 minutes or until bubbly.

Yield: 4 to 6 servings.

Nashville's own songbird, Dinah Shore, made her first appearance at the Ryman at her graduation from Hume-Fogg High School. She subsequently made several appearances there in a career in which she built a national reputation in the recording industry, radio and film. She taped her award-winning television series at the Ryman, appearing with Minnie Pearl, Roy Acuff and Eddy Arnold.

F R O M   G R A N D M O T H E R ' S   C O O K B O O K

Squash

Peel and quarter three common sized squash, cover with water, and let them boil until perfectly tender. Drain off the water, pour them into a bowl, add, when nearly cool, three eggs, one tablespoon of sugar, one tablespoon of butter, a little salt, enough flour to make a thick batter, and fry in hot lard.

Bluegrass music, growing out of the 1950's and 1960's revival of folk music, has a special place at the Ryman, where bluegrass nights, sponsored by Martha White, are still celebrated by some of its earliest proponents as well as newer converts. Bill Monroe's definition of bluegrass is emotional: "It's got a hard drive to it. It's Scotch bagpipes and ole-time fiddlin'. It's Methodist and Holiness and Baptist. It's plain music that tells a good story. It's played from my heart to your heart, and it will touch you. Bluegrass is a music that matters. It's not a music you play, get it over, and forget it."

Chicken Cordon Bluegrass

Take a lesson from Bill Monroe's revivals of old favorites, and try this updated version of chicken with country ham.

8 chicken breast halves, skinned, boned
8 thin slices country ham
8 slices Swiss cheese
3 tablespoons chopped parsley
¼ teaspoon pepper
2 eggs, beaten
1 cup Italian bread crumbs
¼ cup margarine
1 (10-ounce) can cream of chicken soup
1 cup sour cream

Bill Monroe

Rinse the chicken and pat dry. Pound ¼ inch thick with a meat mallet. Top each chicken fillet with a slice of ham and cheese; sprinkle with the parsley and pepper. Roll the chicken to enclose the filling; secure with wooden picks. Dip the rolls in the eggs and roll in the bread crumbs. Brown in the margarine in a large heavy skillet. Remove to a 9x13-inch baking dish. Stir the soup and sour cream into the drippings in the skillet. Pour over the chicken.

Bake at 350 degrees for 45 minutes.

Yield: 8 servings.

Photograph courtesy of Donnie Beauchamp

Yeast Rolls

This recipe comes from Earl and Louise Scruggs.

> 1 cup warm water
> 2 envelopes dry yeast
> 1 egg
> ¼ cup sugar
> 1 teaspoon salt
> ¼ cup shortening
> Flour

Pour the warm water over the yeast in a bowl and let stand for 2 minutes. Add the egg, sugar, salt, shortening and 1 cup flour. Stir and beat until smooth. Add flour until the mixture forms a soft dough, mixing well after each addition. Place in a greased bowl, turning to coat the surface. Let rise, covered, in a warm place for 2 hours or until doubled in bulk. Roll ¼ inch thick on a floured surface. Shape as desired into rolls. Place in a greased baking pan. Let rise until doubled in bulk. Bake at 400 degrees until golden brown.

Yield: 6 dozen.

Lester Flatt and Earl Scruggs and the Foggy Mountain Boys bring bluegrass and Martha White to thousands of listeners from the stage of the Ryman.

Photograph courtesy of Grand Ole Opry Archives

Lester Flatt and Earl Scruggs began with Bill Monroe's Blue Grass Boys, but soon went on to become superstars of bluegrass music in their own right. Earl Scruggs is honored to have been on the first televised program at the Ryman after its renovation, performing with Vince Gill and Marty Stuart in a CBS program called "Roots of Country: Nashville Celebrates the Ryman." His favorite memory may be of receiving an encore in 1969 when he performed "Foggy Mountain Breakdown" with his sons, Gary, Randy and Steve.

The Jordanaires have performed at the Ryman in a variety of musical styles, including country, pop and spiritual, and have provided background harmony for hit recordings by such stars as Patsy Cline, Ricky Nelson and Elvis Presley, who came to the Ryman at their invitation in 1957. About the Ryman they say, "There was something very vital about the Ryman that we hated to leave behind. Sometimes we wonder have we ever sounded as good as we sounded there. The audience sounded great there, too...there was such a feel at the Ryman we wonder if maybe we left some of our spirit there. We love that Ryman."

Best Chocolate Syrup Brownies

The Jordanaires agree that this is their favorite recipe. It is quick and easy to make.

½ cup butter, softened
1 cup sugar
3 eggs
Salt to taste
1 cup flour
¾ cup chocolate syrup
2 teaspoons vanilla extract
¾ cup chopped walnuts or pecans

Cream the butter and sugar in a mixer bowl until light and fluffy. Beat in the eggs. Add the salt and flour, mixing well. Stir in the chocolate syrup, vanilla and walnuts. Spoon into a greased and lightly floured 9x9-inch baking pan and smooth the top.

Bake at 350 degrees for 35 minutes or until a wooden pick inserted near the center comes out clean. Cool on a wire rack. Cut into squares. Garnish with additional walnuts or pecans halves or dust with confectioners' sugar.

Yield: 16 servings.

The Jordanaires, left to right: Hoyt Hawkins, Ray Walker, Neal Matthews, and Gordon Stoker in front

Elvis Presley

Peanut Butter and Banana Sandwiches

This favorite recipe of Elvis Presley is from Elvis in Hollywood: Recipes Fit For a King, *Copyright 1994 by Elizabeth McKeon. Published by Rutledge Hill Press, Nashville, Tennessee.*

> ¼ cup creamy peanut butter
> 2 very ripe bananas, mashed
> 10 slices buttered bread
> Butter

Blend the peanut butter and the bananas in a medium bowl until smooth. Spread on the unbuttered side of half the bread slices and top with the remaining bread. Melt enough butter in a skillet to cover the bottom of the pan. Add the sandwiches. Fry until lightly toasted on both sides; drain on paper towels.

Yield: 5 servings.

Many stories abound about Elvis Presley's 1954 appearance at the Ryman. Justin Tubb remembers that he wore red satin pants and a drugstore cowboy shirt and that he didn't go over too well, because country music fans weren't quite ready for him. Presley's guitarist Scotty Moore recalls the evening much the same as Tubb, recalling that Elvis sang both sides of the record, "That's All Right" and "Blue Moon of Kentucky." "On a scale of one to ten I'd say it was something like a five — with an anchor."

Left to right: Waylon Jennings, Hal Ketchum, Neil Diamond, Tim McGraw, and Raul Malo

Neil Diamond, who played at the Ryman in 1972, returned in 1996 for a taping of his TV special "Neil Diamond... Under a Tennessee Moon." The special finale, "Kentucky Woman," is a holdover from one of the earlier Ryman appearances and appears on an album he recorded in Nashville. At this Ryman appearance, it included guest appearances by Waylon Jennings, Raul Malo of The Mavericks, Hal Ketchum and Tim McGraw, who was only five years old when Diamond performed at the Auditorium in 1972.

Beef Pot Roast

Neil recommends serving Gedempte Fleish, or Beef Pot Roast, with potato pancakes or kasha varnishkas. He also likes to crumble matzo into a bowl and ladle the gravy from the pot roast over it.

    2 (2-pound) slices chuck roast
    1 envelope onion soup mix
    1 cup water
    1 teaspoon minced garlic
    Salt and pepper to taste
    6 potatoes, cut into quarters
    1 green bell pepper, cut into quarters
    6 carrots, cut into quarters
    2 ribs celery, cut into quarters
    Catsup to taste

Trim the beef and cut into bite-size pieces. Combine the onion soup mix with the water in a large skillet. Add the beef and garlic and sprinkle with salt and pepper. Simmer, covered, for 1 hour. Layer the potatoes, green pepper, carrots and celery over the beef and drizzle with catsup. Simmer for 1½ hours longer.

Yield: 5 to 6 servings.

Photograph courtesy of Neal Preston

Devilish Love Bars

Robin, wife of Marty Roe, the lead singer of Diamond Rio, says that these are Marty's all-time favorites.

2 cups flour
2 cups sugar
1 teaspoon baking soda
2 eggs, beaten
½ cup buttermilk
2 teaspoons vanilla extract
1 cup margarine
¼ cup baking cocoa
1 cup water
½ cup buttermilk
½ cup margarine
1 (1-pound) package confectioners' sugar
½ cup baking cocoa
Finely chopped nuts (optional)

Left to right: Jimmy Olander, Brian Prout, Gene Johnson, Dana Williams, Dan Truman, and Marty Roe

Mix the flour, sugar and baking soda in a bowl. Add the eggs, ½ cup buttermilk and vanilla and mix well. Combine 1 cup margarine, ¼ cup baking cocoa and water in a saucepan. Bring to a boil, stirring to blend well. Add to the batter and mix well. Spoon into a greased and floured 12x15-inch baking pan.

Bake at 350 degrees for 20 minutes or until set. Bring ½ cup buttermilk and ½ cup margarine to a boil in a saucepan. Add the confectioners' sugar, ½ cup baking cocoa and nuts and mix well. Pour over the hot baked layer. Let stand until cool. Cut into bars.

Yield: 5 dozen.

Photograph courtesy of Brett Lopez

Diamond Rio is an example of the vibrant new talent that is appearing at the Ryman since its renovation. Their program included country, bluegrass and gospel tunes, showcasing the band's instrumental and vocal capabilities. Dana Williams, bass singer and resident humorist, reminisced about coming to the Ryman years ago with his grandfather. He thanked the Hanes company for sponsoring the band, but added that he had waited too long to appear at the Ryman to stand there talking about underwear.

Opening night of the weekly Martha White Bluegrass Night concert series at the Ryman featured Alison Krauss, one of the rising stars of bluegrass music, who Bill Monroe introduced as "a wonderful singer and a fine fiddle player." In 1993, she had become the youngest cast member of the Grand Ole Opry and the first bluegrass act added to the roster since 1964.

Of the Ryman, Alison says "We couldn't believe we were there, standing on the same stage and playing and singing through the same microphones as all those great artists we'd heard on the radio even before we started playing music."

Corn Bread

This is Alison's own recipe for winning corn bread. She makes it with Martha White corn meal mix and flour, sponsor of the bluegrass nights at the Ryman.

> 1 tablespoon bacon drippings or vegetable oil
> ¾ cup self-rising corn meal mix
> ¼ cup self-rising flour
> 1 tablespoon sugar
> 1 egg, beaten
> 1 cup buttermilk
> 3 tablespoons vegetable oil

Preheat the oven to 450 degrees. Grease an 8-inch skillet with the bacon drippings and place it in the oven to heat. Combine the corn meal mix, flour and sugar in a medium bowl. Stir in the egg, buttermilk and oil. Sprinkle a small amount of additional cornmeal into the hot skillet and pour in the batter.

Bake for 10 to 15 minutes or until golden brown. May double recipe and bake in a 10-inch skillet for 25 minutes; bake corn sticks or muffins for 10 to 15 minutes.

Yield: 4 to 6 servings.

Alison Krauss with Barry Bales on acoustic bass

Photograph courtesy of Donnie Beauchamp

Chicken Pickin' Corn Soup

This is a favorite of Ricky's, which he has shared with us.

3 or 4 boneless skinless chicken breasts
Salt, pepper and McCormick chicken seasoning to taste
5 tablespoons vegetable oil
1 (10-ounce) can cream of chicken soup
1 (10-ounce) can cream of mushroom soup
1 (10-ounce) soup can water
4 medium potatoes, chopped
2 medium onions, chopped
1 (16-ounce) can whole kernel corn
1 (16-ounce) can cream-style corn
1½ tablespoons cornstarch
1 cup water

Rinse the chicken and cut into bite-size pieces. Sprinkle with salt, pepper and chicken seasoning. Brown on all sides in the oil in a saucepan. Remove the chicken. Stir in the soups and 1 soup can of water. Bring to a boil. Add the potatoes, onions and corn. Bring to a boil and add the chicken. Blend the cornstarch with 1 cup water and stir into the saucepan. Simmer for 45 to 60 minutes or until the vegetables are tender, stirring occasionally.

Yield: 8 servings.

Ricky Skaggs (center) with Bill Monroe and Tom Ewing, a member of Bill Monroe's Bluegrass Boys

Photograph courtesy of Donnie Beauchamp

Ricky Skaggs, Grammy winner and multi-instrumentalist, hosts "CMT Presents Monday Night Concerts at the Ryman." The concerts reflect the range of music that the Ryman has nurtured, with a blend of country, pop, rhythm and blues, bluegrass and gospel. Ricky remembers a trip to the Ryman when he was seven years old. "I still remember vividly the sights, sounds and smells...the smell of Juicy Fruit and sweat, body sweat, and I can remember the sounds of the steel guitar playing and hitting the ceiling and bouncing all around and the colors of the suits...They are pretty awesome memories."

The Ryman Auditorium celebrated Tennessee's bicentennial with two special concerts in May of 1996. "Guitar Town Comes Alive" featured world-class guitar players Steve Wariner, Larry Carlton and Leo Kottke, and the legendary Chet Atkins, who is largely responsible for the creation of the Nashville sound. "Rock and Country Collide" continued the celebration with a focus on the rockabilly sounds of Memphis and the more traditional country roots of East Tennessee and featured Jerry Lee Lewis and Mandy Barnett. Kelly Tolson, executive director of Tennessee 200, Inc., says that "These great talents and the unique Ryman setting (added) another spontaneous, even explosive ingredient to Tennessee's bicentennial celebration."

Mushroom Crust Quiche

McConnell's Catering has catered backstage events for the artists performing at the Ryman and shares this recipe, which can be cut into very small pieces to serve as an appetizer. Even "real men" will eat this quiche.

8 ounces mushrooms, coarsely chopped
3 tablespoons butter
½ cup fine cracker crumbs
¾ cup finely chopped green onions
2 tablespoons butter
2 cups shredded Swiss cheese
1 cup cottage cheese
4 eggs
¼ teaspoon cayenne
¼ teaspoon paprika

Sauté the mushrooms in 3 tablespoons butter in a skillet over medium heat until tender. Stir in the cracker crumbs. Press the mixture over the bottom and side of a greased 9-inch pie plate. Sauté the green onions in 2 tablespoons butter in the same skillet until transparent. Spread the green onions and Swiss cheese in the shell. Process the cottage cheese, eggs and cayenne in a blender until smooth. Pour into the prepared dish and sprinkle with paprika.

Bake at 350 degrees for 20 to 25 minutes or until a knife inserted near the center comes out clean. Let stand for 10 to 15 minutes before serving.

Steve Wariner

Yield: 6 servings.

Photograph courtesy of Ron Keith

Broccoli Cheese Soup

This recipe is from the kitchen of songwriter Randy Goodrum and his wife Gail.

1 bunch broccoli, about
    1¼ pounds
Salt to taste
2 medium onions, sliced
3 tablespoons butter
7 cups chicken broth
1 teaspoon oregano leaves
¼ cup flour
2 tablespoons melted
    butter
2 tablespoons Dijon mustard
⅓ teaspoon pepper
1 cup milk
2 cups shredded Cheddar cheese

Pictured at the Ryman's Tin Pan South '96 "Legendary Songwriters Acoustic Concert" are John D. Loudermilk, John Phillips, Michael Masser, Janis Ian, Association President Pat Alger, Roger Cook, Randy Goodrum, Host Fred Knobloch, John Sebastian and Allen Toussaint. The concert climaxes an annual week-long music festival celebrating songwriters.

Cut the broccoli florets from the stalks; peel and chop the stalks. Simmer the broccoli florets in lightly salted water to cover in a saucepan for 2 to 3 minutes; drain and set aside. Sauté the chopped broccoli stalks with the onions in 3 tablespoons butter in a large saucepan for 5 minutes. Add 3 cups of the broth and oregano. Simmer for 20 to 30 minutes or until the vegetables are tender. Process in a blender or food processor until smooth.

Blend the flour into 2 tablespoons melted butter in a large saucepan. Cook until bubbly, stirring frequently. Stir in the mustard, pepper, puréed mixture and remaining 4 cups broth. Bring to a simmer, stirring constantly. Add the milk and cheese. Simmer until the cheese melts, stirring constantly. Add the broccoli florets. Cook just until heated through.

Yield: 8 servings.

CENTER STAGE

...SHOWCASING THE STARS

A tradition for great theater at the Ryman was established as early as 1906, when the legendary Sarah Bernhardt's special train rolled into Nashville bringing her entire Parisian company. They had come to do *Camille*.

Thereafter, the Ryman stage saw a parade of famous actors, actresses, and dancers who came either to perform or to speak. Alf and Robert Taylor were among the earliest. Rudolph Valentino, Charlie Chaplin, Mary Pickford, and Douglas Fairbanks all made appearances here as speakers, some for specific causes.

Mary Pickford

The Ryman continued to enjoy theater in the golden years before radio and movies, serving as the only venue in town large enough for plays to try out "on the road" before moving on to the city. The auditorium was even able to survive the lean years for theater on the road. In a 1939 article in *The New York Time Magazine*, Brock Pemberton cites Nashville's Tabernacle as a symbol of the theater that survived the Depression and the advent of movies intact — due in large part to "Mrs. Elsie Naff, America's most picturesque manageress."

Mrs. Naff's formula for success included bringing in the big stars and the big plays. Over a thirty-year period, she brought in such big-name stars as Gertrude Lawrence, Judith Anderson, Walter Huston, Bela Lugosi, Alfred Lunt, Lynn Fontanne, Joe E. Brown, Harpo Marx, Mae West, Maurice Evans, Greer Garson, and Irene Castle, among others.

Some were not such big names when they appeared at the Ryman, but certainly distinguished themselves later. Among those were Doris Day, Tyrone Power, ZaSu Pitts, Orson Welles, Basil Rathbone, and Ethel Waters.

Tallulah Bankhead played in *Reflected Glory* and *The Little Foxes*, and Helen Hayes starred in *Mary of Scotland* and *Victoria Regina*. In 1941, no less a cast than Katharine Hepburn, Van Heflin, and Joseph Cotten assembled for *The Philadelphia Story* as enthralled patrons lined the

Chorus girls in a makeshift dressing room with pews and curtains
Photograph courtesy of F. Robinson Collection, Vanderbilt University Library

I first worked at the
Ryman in '46.
Good sound remains...by
far the best sound in
town! Maybe the U.S.
—Chet Atkins

Greer Garson

Ryman's aisles and back walls. In the sixties, traveling Broadway productions like *The Sound of Music* starring Mary Martin, kept the tradition going.

Vaudeville companies loved the Ryman, bringing, among others, The Ziegfeld Follies with Fanny Brice, Billie Burke, and Eve Arden in the company.

Dance was also a regular on the roster here. Legendary dancers Isadora Duncan, Anna Pavlova, Martha Graham, and Jose Greco all performed here, as did the world-renowned Ballet Russe. In 1961, when the Ryman planned its 70th birthday celebration, it wasn't country music on stage. It was the American Ballet Theatre. That was a particularly gala evening for the old tabernacle, with gas lights in the sidewalks, antique cars at the curb, and a canopy over the red carpet leading guests up to the doors.

Of all the big acts booked into the Ryman through the years, Bob Hope proved to be the biggest. Hope's appearance in 1949 with Doris Day and the Les Brown Band broke all attendance and receipt records to date.

About the then-aging auditorium, Hope mused, "What an amazing garage this is! When do the bats fly out?"

Photograph courtesy of F. Robinson Collection, Vanderbilt University Library

Pavlova

The Pavlova was created by Chef Bert Sachse of Perth's Esplanade Hotel in honor of one of the hotel's most distinguished guests, the Russian prima ballerina, Anna Pavlova. It has since become an Australian national dish.

4 egg whites
Salt to taste
1¼ cups superfine sugar
1 teaspoon vinegar
2 teaspoons cornflour or cornstarch
Whipped cream
Strawberries
Sliced kiwifruit
Sliced passion fruit
Sliced bananas

Anna Pavlova

Draw an 8-inch circle on baking parchment and brush with oil. Place on a greased baking sheet. Beat the egg whites with salt in a mixer bowl until stiff but not dry. Add the sugar 1 tablespoon at a time, beating constantly until the meringue is glossy. Sprinkle with the vinegar and cornflour and fold in gently. Spread evenly over the oiled circle, making a depression in the center with the back of the spoon.

Place on a rack in the bottom half of an oven preheated to 350 degrees. Reduce the oven temperature to 250 degrees. Bake for 1½ hours. Turn off the heat. Let the meringue stand in the closed oven until cool. Remove the meringue to a serving plate. Fill with whipped cream and top with strawberries, kiwifruit, passion fruit and bananas.

Yield: 12 servings.

One of the most glamorous figures to appear at the Ryman in the early days was the famous Russian ballerina Anna Pavlova, who appeared there four times. Despite her legendary beauty and fame, manager Naff found her to be a woman who put on no airs at all. Naff was quoted in the newspaper at the time as saying, "She always came three or four days ahead of her engagement, walked a great deal, lived very simply and put on no grand manners with us at the auditorium."

Russian Mushroom Salad

The original recipe for this Russian dish calls for orange-agaric mushrooms, but says that it can be prepared with ordinary button mushrooms. It would have been a welcome treat for the Pavley-Oukrainsky Ballet in 1920.

1 pound mushrooms, coarsely chopped
Juice of 1 lemon
Salt and pepper to taste
¼ cup butter
1 cup herbed wine vinegar
2 shallots, chopped
½ cup vegetable oil
2 tablespoons chopped chives
½ cup sour cream or plain
    yogurt
½ teaspoon sugar
1 teaspoon paprika

Sauté the mushrooms with the lemon juice, salt and pepper in the butter in a saucepan. Let stand until cool. Combine the vinegar, shallots, oil, chives, sour cream, sugar and paprika in a bowl and mix well. Add the mushrooms and mix gently. Chill until serving time. Serve on lettuce-lined plates as a salad or hors d'oeuvre.

Yield: 6 servings.

The Pavley–Oukrainsky Russian Ballet, which appeared at the Ryman in 1920, assured Mrs. Naff that "the performance to be given in your city will be a memorable event and do a great credit to you." Management had very specific instructions regarding the need for an orchestra for twenty–six. "When in doubt leave the first rows unsold until our arrival and when necessary have the rows removed."

Art courtesy of F. Robinson Collection, Vanderbilt University Library

Beef Stroganoff

Patrons eager to entertain the Ballet Russe may have offered them this version of a Russian favorite.

1½ pounds top sirloin
Salt and pepper to taste
2 small onions, sliced
1½ tablespoons butter
1 tablespoon flour
1½ tablespoons melted butter
1 cup beef bouillon
¾ teaspoon prepared spicy mustard
3 tablespoons (or more) sour cream,
    at room temperature

Trim the beef and cut into ½ x 2-inch strips; sprinkle with salt and pepper. Brown the beef with the onions in 1½ tablespoons heated butter in a saucepan. Blend the flour into 1½ tablespoons melted butter in a medium saucepan. Add the bouillon. Cook until thickened, stirring constantly. Stir in the mustard and sour cream. Add the beef and onions. Heat over low heat for 20 minutes; do not boil. Serve over noodles if desired. Garnish with paprika.

Yield: 6 servings.

The Ballet Russe de Monte Carlo was just as confident of their billing as the Pavley–Oukrainsky Russian Ballet, advertising "Twenty Five Ballets, Company of 125, Symphony Orchestra — the only genuine Russian ballet company in this country which carries on the glamorous traditions of a thrilling stage art...a spectacle that has been riotously greeted in every cultural center of Europe and America!" Records indicate that their performance of "Prince Igor" was well, if not riotously, received at the Ryman.

Poster courtesy of Nashville Room, Nashville and Davidson County Library

The Ryman also hosted one of the most controversial dancers of her era, Isadora Duncan. Although Duncan was an American, she lived abroad most of her career and the troupe that she brought to the Ryman was billed as the Isadora Duncan Dancers from Moscow. Duncan, strongly influenced by the art of Greece, often danced barefoot in a loose Greek tunic. She rebelled against the formal training of classical ballet and encouraged an individual style of expression that has greatly influenced modern dance in America.

Dolmathes

This classical Greek dish would have been familiar to Isadora Duncan in her pursuit of the Greek culture that influenced her dancing. It can be served as an appetizer as well as a main dish.

1 pound lean ground beef
1 egg, beaten
1 medium onion, finely chopped
½ cup uncooked rice
¼ cup chopped parsley
1 teaspoon chopped fresh mint
2 tablespoons olive oil
¼ cup water
Salt and pepper to taste
Fresh or canned grape leaves or cabbage leaves
1½ cups each beef bouillon and water
2 eggs
Juice of 1 lemon

Combine the first 10 ingredients in a bowl and mix well. Soak fresh grape leaves or cabbage leaves in hot water for 5 minutes to soften; rinse canned grape leaves in warm water. Place grape leaves shiny side down on a work surface. Place a spoonful of the beef mixture on each grape leaf and roll to enclose the filling, tucking in the ends to seal well. Place seam side down in a saucepan, making several layers if necessary. Add the bouillon and 1½ cups water. Simmer, covered, for 45 minutes. Beat 2 eggs with the lemon juice in a bowl. Add a small amount of the hot cooking broth, beating constantly. Stir the egg mixture into the remaining cooking broth. Let stand, covered, for 5 minutes to thicken. Serve with the dolmathes.

Yield: 6 servings.

Art courtesy of F. Robinson Collection, Vanderbilt University Library

Martha Grahams

*Martha might never have sampled this dish,
which is here named for her, but she would
doubtless have approved.*

10 to 12 whole graham crackers
1 cup butter
1 cup packed brown sugar
1 cup chopped pecans

Martha Graham

Arrange the graham crackers in a single layer in a 9x13-inch baking
pan. Bring the butter and brown sugar to a boil in a saucepan, stirring
occasionally. Boil for 3 minutes, stirring occasionally. Remove from
the heat and stir in the pecans. Pour over the graham crackers.

Bake at 325 degrees for 10 minutes. Cut into squares while still warm
and remove to a wire rack to cool.

Yield: 20 servings.

*Martha Graham, the
famous pioneer of modern
dance, was influenced by
Greek mythology, but later
moved on to interpret
American life, including a
theme closer to the hearts of
Tennesseans, her joyous
"Appalachian Spring." She
was well received by Ryman
audiences, who apparently
were not shocked by
her expression of the baser
emotions such as fear,
jealousy, anger and hatred and
with her sometimes
sharp, angular poses and
abrupt, jerky actions.*

George Pullen Jackson in his review in the Nashville Banner indicated that the 1929 performance of Ted Shawn, Ruth St. Denis, and the Denishawn Dancers carried terpsichorean art to new heights. The article tells us that the dancers were forced to repeat three of their dance numbers because they were so enthusiastically received by the audience. Mr. Jackson was impressed by their dance interpretation and posturing and by Ruth St. Denis' "draperies." As for the costumes of Ted Shawn, "there is little to say, for there was so little of them. He is an Apollo. And such gods use no clothing."

Exotic Shrimp Salad

Only an exotic salad would do justice to the atmosphere created by the Denishawn Dancers, who drew much of their inspiration from the Asian subcontinent. This can be served as a first course or an appetizer.

1 cup shredded coconut
2 cups milk
1 pound shrimp
1 bay leaf
10 whole cloves
1 teaspoon sugar
Salt to taste
8 shallots, chopped
2 cloves of garlic, sliced
2 tablespoons vegetable oil
1 apple, grated
1 tablespoon soy sauce
1 green bell pepper, chopped
5 tablespoons peanuts
Pepper to taste

The Denishawn Dancers

Bring the coconut to a boil in the milk in a saucepan and remove from the heat; let stand for 1 hour. Press through a sieve or squeeze in a cheesecloth, reserving the juice. Discard the coconut or reserve for another use. Combine the shrimp with water to cover, bay leaf, cloves, sugar and salt. Bring to a boil and remove from the heat. Let stand for 10 minutes; drain, discarding the bay leaf and cloves. Sauté the shallots and garlic lightly in the oil in a skillet; cool. Mix with the remaining ingredients and coconut milk in a bowl. Add the shrimp and mix lightly. Chill until serving time. Serve on lettuce-lined plates.

Yield: 6 servings.

Photograph courtesy of F. Robinson Collection, Vanderbilt University Library

Creamy Potato Soup

Doubtless the dancers and audience alike would have been glad of a hearty and warming bowl of soup while waiting for the curtain to go up on that cold night in January when the Joos Ballet performed.

4 cups chopped potatoes
1 cup sliced celery
1 cup chopped onion
2 to 3 cups water
2 teaspoons salt
1 cup milk
1 cup half-and-half
1 tablespoon butter
1 tablespoon parsley flakes
Pepper to taste

Combine the potatoes, celery, onion, water and salt in a large saucepan. Simmer, covered, for 20 minutes or until the vegetables are tender; remove from the heat. Mash the potatoes coarsely with a fork. Stir in the milk, half-and-half, butter, parsley flakes and pepper. Heat just to a simmer; do not boil. May add ½ teaspoon caraway seeds if desired.

Yield: 6 to 8 servings.

FROM GRANDMOTHER'S COOKBOOK

Potato Soup

One quart milk, one stalk of celery, one small onion, four potatoes, boiled and mashed, one tablespoonful of butter, and one of flour creamed in. Add salt to taste. Put through a sieve, and serve in a hot tureen.

Not all performances at the Ryman were unqualified successes. Nijinsky danced for a very small audience under the watchful eye of Serge Diaghilev, who stood in the wings. The Joos Ballet, which performed "Coppelia" in 1946, fell afoul of the season when a very cold night in January kept Nashville crowds at home. The company refused to go on without their $1,000, which was not in the "box." Mrs. Naff wrote that "Later the company went to Europe and I think cancelled the debt...It was after nine when the curtain went up to a small audience. I didn't even look in."

Old-Fashioned Fudge

This is Donna Rizzo's grandma's fudge. She says to be sure to use a large black skillet and rub the rim with butter to keep the mixture from boiling over.

⅔ cup baking cocoa
3 cups sugar
1½ cups milk prepared from dry milk powder
1 teaspoon vanilla extract
¼ cup butter

Mix the baking cocoa and sugar in a large black skillet. Add the milk. Bring to a boil over medium heat, stirring constantly. Cook to 234 to 240 degrees on a candy thermometer, soft-ball stage; do not stir.

Remove from the heat and stir in the vanilla and butter. Beat until the mixture thickens and loses its gloss. Pour into a buttered 8- or 9-inch glass dish. Let stand for 1 hour. Cut into pieces.

Yield: 16 servings.

The Ryman still hosts dance, with a 1994 performance by the Tennessee Dance Theatre. This performance, "Quilts," is based, appropriately enough, on patterns in both quilts and Tennessee life and won the Tennessee Governor's Award for Excellence in Dance. Donna Rizzo, artistic director with Andrew Krichels, says that dancing at the Ryman was the highlight of her performing experience. "My Minnie Pearl solo was premiered on the very stage that Minnie considered her HOME for over forty years. Her presence, I know, was with me that evening, for I've never danced better."

Tennessee Dance Theatre

Photograph by Jim DeVault

Sarah Bernhardt

Gateau au Chocolat

Even Camille might have risen from her deathbed for this flourless French cake.

  9 tablespoons unsalted butter, sliced
  11 ounces semisweet chocolate, coarsely chopped
  9 egg yolks
  2½ ounces chopped pecans
  9 egg whites
  6 tablespoons sugar

Line the bottom of a buttered 10-inch cake pan with baking parchment; butter and flour the parchment. Melt the butter in a saucepan over low heat. Add the chocolate. Heat until the chocolate melts, stirring to blend well; remove from the heat. Stir in the egg yolks and pecans. Beat the egg whites in a mixer bowl until stiff peaks form. Blend in the sugar. Fold gradually into the chocolate mixture. Spoon into the prepared cake pan.

Bake at 250 degrees for 1 hour or until a wooden pick inserted in the center comes out clean. Cool on a wire rack.

Yield: 8 servings.

Sarah Bernhardt's 1906 appearance at the Ryman was the first of many grand theatrical events at the Auditorium. Two rows of seats were removed at that time to extend the stage and square it off at the front. Although dressing rooms were planned, they never materialized and curtains hid the dressing space, with performers putting on make-up in pews. Sarah arrived with her Parisian troupe in her special railroad car. Although sixty-one years of age and speaking French, she was able to completely captivate the audience of more than three thousand people with her re-creation of the tragic death of Camille and played to bravas and grand acclaim.

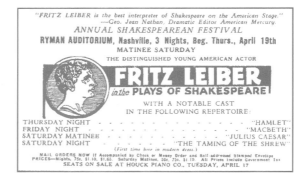

Shakespeare was a perennial favorite at the Ryman and constituted the standard theater fare during the teens and twenties. In 1926, audiences could see Fritz Leiber or Robert B. Mantell and Genevieve Hamper in a different Shakespearian play every night for a week, including "Hamlet" in modern dress on Tuesday for as little as fifty cents. Alfred Lunt and Lynn Fontanne appeared in "The Taming of the Shrew" in the forties, although the boilers broke down for the January performance and Naff reported that only "by firing all night and with plumbers helping we got the house warm."

Hamlets

Serve these miniature ham sandwiches in modern dress at your next party.

> *½ cup butter*
> *2 tablespoons onion flakes*
> *1½ teaspoons dry mustard*
> *1 teaspoon Worcestershire sauce*
> *1½ teaspoons poppy seeds*
> *2 (24-count) packages small dinner rolls*
> *1½ pounds thinly sliced cooked ham*
> *16 ounces Swiss cheese, thinly sliced*

Combine the butter, onion flakes, dry mustard, Worcestershire sauce and poppy seeds in a small saucepan. Heat until the butter melts, stirring to mix well. Slice the dinner rolls horizontally into 2 layers; do not separate the rolls. Layer the ham and cheese on each of the bottom layers and replace the top layers. Replace the rolls in the foil roll pans. Pour the butter mixture over the top.

Bake at 350 degrees for 20 minutes. Cut into individual sandwiches.

Yield: 4 dozen.

Poster courtesy of Nashville Room, Nashville and Davidson County Library

78

Mascarpone and Walnut Pasta

Portia and the merchant of Venice might have enjoyed this creamy and crunchy Italian dish.

> 1 clove of garlic, crushed
> ¼ cup butter
> 1¾ cups chopped walnuts
> 1 cup plus 2 tablespoons mascarpone cheese
> ½ cup grated Parmesan cheese
> Salt and freshly ground pepper to taste
> 16 ounces penne, cooked al dente

Sauté the garlic in the butter in a heavy saucepan over medium heat for 30 seconds or just until golden brown. Add the walnuts. Sauté for 3 to 4 minutes. Stir in the mascarpone cheese. Heat until the cheese melts, stirring constantly. Fold in the Parmesan cheese, salt and pepper. Combine with the pasta in a serving bowl and toss gently to mix well.

Yield: 6 servings.

Maude Adams also played Shakespeare to Ryman audiences with her 1932 performance of Portia opposite Otis Skinner in "The Merchant of Venice." Adams, no longer young in 1932 and with a celebrated theater career behind her, had threatened not to appear if there were no running water in her dressing room. Little did she know that were it not for her threat she would not even have had a dressing room. Mrs. Naff had a small room built according to her specifications, which later became the exclusive property of the male stars of the Opry.

MAUDE
ADAMS
AND
OTIS
SKINNER

IN

William Shakespeare's Comedy
"THE MERCHANT OF VENICE"

Under the Management of
ERLANGER PRODUCTIONS, Inc.

RYMAN AUDITORIUM
NASHVILLE, TENN.
One Night Only
SATURDAY, JANUARY 23rd

Program courtesy of F. Robinson Collection, Vanderbilt University Library

Tom Ryman and Sam Jones might have had some uneasy moments had they been around when "Tobacco Road" came to the Ryman. There was quite a bit of controversy over the booking, with the Nashville newspapers leading the charge. In a letter to Francis Robinson, Naff reported, "Well, I am still alive, and 'Tobacco Road' has been and gone, so they can't put me in jail." She went on to say that the capacity crowd "knew what kind of a play it was, and many buying tickets had seen it before and most of them had read the book, so no one was surprised or disappointed."

Turnip Greens

The residents of Tobacco Road were certainly familiar with turnip greens; these are served up with an uptown flavor.

> 1½ pounds turnip greens
> 1 teaspoon salt
> ½ to ¾ cup water
> 4 slices bacon
> 2 tablespoons finely chopped onion
> 2 tablespoons cider vinegar
> Pepper to taste
> 2 hard-cooked eggs, chopped

Wash the turnip greens 4 or 5 times, discarding the tough stems. Cook, covered, in the salted water for 45 minutes or until tender. Fry the bacon in a skillet until crisp; drain and crumble the bacon, reserving 2 tablespoons of the drippings in the skillet. Sauté the onion lightly in the bacon drippings; remove from the heat. Stir in the vinegar. Drain the turnip greens and adjust the seasonings; place in a serving bowl. Pour the drippings mixture over the turnip greens. Top with the bacon and chopped eggs.

Yield: 4 to 6 servings.

Poster courtesy of Nashville Room, Nashville and Davidson County Library

This oil painting of the Ryman depicts its early days as the Union Gospel Tabernacle. It shows the now lost crest tiles, a row of stylized flowers, similar to the ones at England's Exeter Cathedral, along the main roof line, and ornamental crockets on the gables. The painting hangs in the renovated Auditorium.

Samuel Porter Jones, on the left, was the fiery evangelist whose revival message inspired Tom Ryman to refocus his life on the Lord's work. Captain Tom Ryman, on the right, owned the Ryman Line Riverboat Company and was the driving force behind the building of the Union Gospel Tabernacle. It was later renamed as a tribute to his work toward its completion.

The Ryman's Fifth Avenue vestibule features an antique radio collection which plays recorded narrations of the early days of WSM radio. Other displays in the auditorium include costumes of many of the Grand Ole Opry stars with early photographs and programs. One exhibit details the life and times of Tom Ryman, while another features Lula Naff and posters of many of the artists she brought to the Ryman.

The balcony is known as the Confederate Gallery. Although its design was included in Hugh Thompson's original plans, it was not built until 1897. The occasion was the reunion of the Confederate Veterans Association — a reunion that brought nearly 100,000 people into Nashville as part of the Tennessee Centennial Exposition.

The Confederate Gallery has been renovated to its original splendor. The original building
committee accepted a low bid of about $10,000 for the iron and steel construction,
the woodwork, and enough seating for 2,500 people. The Louisville Bridge Company did the
iron work, anchoring the structure with steel columns extending to the basement.

The oak pews in the Ryman Auditorium bask in the afternoon sunlight
that filters through the original stained glass windows.
The pews were built by the Indiana Church Furnishing Company.
Before the auditorium reopened in 1994, each pew was
carefully removed and refurbished, readying them for another century.

Roy Acuff and Minnie Pearl, two of the Grand Ole Opry's most beloved performers,

are reunited in this poignant bronze sculpture by Russell Faxon.

They can be found visiting in the renovated Auditorium's Fourth Avenue lobby.

The lights of Nashville's Mother Church once again shine to show the way for its many congregants to gather for evenings of music, dance and drama.

Sinsational Chocolate Cheesecake

This is almost as wicked as Mae West and sure to liven up a dinner party.

1 (8-ounce) package chocolate wafers
⅓ cup melted butter or margarine
2 tablespoons sugar
¼ teaspoon nutmeg
3 eggs
1 cup sugar
24 ounces cream cheese, softened
2 cups semisweet chocolate chips, melted
1 teaspoon vanilla extract
Salt to taste
1 cup sour cream

Ryman audiences also occasionally enjoyed lighter fare in the form of Vaudeville performances. Mae West was the "Sinsational Hit of the Town" in "Diamond Lil" and Anna Held titillated audiences with her famous snow–white bosom and diamond stockings. Later performances included "The High Lights of 1934," Earl Carroll's "Vanities," George White's "Scandals," and the "Ziegfeld Follies."

Process the chocolate wafers in a blender until finely crushed. Mix with the butter, 2 tablespoons sugar and nutmeg in a bowl. Press evenly over the bottom and side of a 9-inch springform pan. Chill in the refrigerator. Combine the eggs and 1 cup sugar in a mixer bowl and beat at high speed until thick and light. Add the cream cheese and beat until smooth. Blend in the melted chocolate, vanilla, salt and sour cream. Pour into the prepared pan.

Bake at 350 degrees for 1 hour or just until firm. Cool in the pan on a wire rack. Chill, covered, for several hours. Place on a serving plate and remove the side of the pan. Garnish with sweetened whipped cream.

Yield: 16 servings.

Poster courtesy of Nashville Room, Nashville and Davidson County Library

The New York Herald Tribune *writer who covered the Ryman appearance of Fannie Brice wrote: "The spectacle of Fannie Brice doing her fan dance in church with an appreciative audience impiously applauding from genuine pews furnished the company (with enjoyment) for months to come." Miss Brice's manager delayed telling her that she would have to dress in a "water closet" until the last minute. When he did, she snapped, "Never mind where I have to dress, how is the house?" Happily, he replied, "It's better than $3,500." "Och," she replied, "for a $3,500 house, I'd dress in a (expletive deleted)." "Well," said the manager, "that's exactly where you are dressing."*

Potato Fans

These are slightly more substantial than the fans Fannie Brice danced with in Billy Rose's "Crazy Quilt."

> 6 medium baking potatoes
> ¼ cup melted butter or margarine
> 1 tablespoon dried chives
> 1 teaspoon tarragon
> 1 teaspoon chervil
> ¾ teaspoon salt
> ½ teaspoon pepper

Fannie Brice

Cut each potato crosswise into ⅛-inch slices, cutting to, but not through, the bottom of the potatoes. Place on a baking sheet. Combine the butter, chives, tarragon, chervil, salt and pepper in a bowl and mix well. Brush over the potatoes.

Bake at 400 degrees for 1 hour or until tender.

Yield: 6 servings.

Photograph courtesy of Nashville Room, Nashville and Davidson County Library

Bela Lugosi

Old Lace Cookies

Be sure to leave the arsenic out of these special cookies.

> ¾ cup finely ground unblanched almonds
> ½ cup butter
> ½ cup sugar
> 1 tablespoon flour
> 1 tablespoon cream
> 1 tablespoon milk

Combine the almonds, butter, sugar, flour, cream and milk in a saucepan. Cook over low heat until the butter melts, stirring constantly to mix well. Drop the mixture by teaspoonfuls 3 inches apart on a greased and floured cookie sheet.

Bake at 350 degrees for 5 minutes or just until slightly brown and bubbly in the center. Cool just until the edges are firm enough to lift with a spatula. Invert onto a paper towel. Roll cookies immediately around the handle of a wooden spoon to shape into tubes.

Yield: 3 dozen.

The determination of Lula Naff continued to make the Ryman a profitable stop for "road" shows, even during the worst times of the Great Depression and World War II. She brought big stars such as Irene Castle, Gertrude Lawrence and Walter Huston, as well as big shows such as "The Student Prince," "Mister Roberts," and "Oklahoma." Bela Lugosi delighted audiences at the Ryman in "Arsenic and Old Lace."

After-the-Theater Shrimp and Pasta Salad

Prepare this main-dish salad early in the day for rave reviews from guests after the theater.

Ethel Barrymore appeared several times at the Ryman. She solved the ongoing problem of no dressing rooms by bringing her own, a portable canvas cubicle, reported to be no larger than a telephone booth. This gave rise to the accusation that it really served as a place to drink between acts, an accusation that Lula Naff stoutly denied. "All this talk of her drinking while she in engaged on the stage makes me angry for I stood within a few feet of her, and found her normal, lovely and gracious."

Florets of 1 bunch broccoli
8 ounces rotini, cooked, drained
1 pound shrimp, cooked
½ cup chopped red or green bell pepper
¼ cup sliced black olives
1 tablespoon sliced green onions
½ cup sour cream
¼ cup mayonnaise
3 tablespoons white wine vinegar
2 tablespoons whipping cream
1½ teaspoons sugar
1 teaspoon tarragon
Salt and pepper to taste

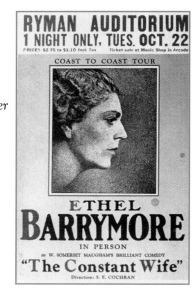

Cook the broccoli in a small amount of boiling water in a saucepan for 3 to 5 minutes or just until tender-crisp; drain. Combine with the pasta, shrimp, bell pepper, olives and green onions in a bowl and mix lightly.

Combine the sour cream, mayonnaise, wine vinegar, cream, sugar, tarragon, salt and pepper in a small bowl and mix well. Add to the salad and toss lightly. Chill, covered, until serving time.

Yield: 4 servings.

Poster courtesy of Nashville Room, Nashville and Davidson County Library

Queen Cakes

Helen Hayes played both Queen Victoria and Mary Queen of Scots at the Ryman. Both would have been familiar with this traditional English recipe.

½ cup butter, softened
½ cup sugar
2 eggs, beaten
½ cup raisins
1 cup sifted self-rising flour
Milk

Cream the butter and sugar in a mixer bowl until light and fluffy. Beat in the eggs gradually. Stir in the raisins. Add the flour and mix well, adding a small amount of milk if necessary to make of the desired consistency. Fill paper-lined muffin cups half full.

Bake at 375 degrees for 15 to 20 minutes or until golden brown. May substitute dates, candied cherries, chocolate chips or crystallized ginger for the raisins.

Yield: 1 dozen.

Helen Hayes probably never forgot her 1938 appearance on the Ryman stage in "Victoria Regina." The famed actress was in the middle of a particularly rousing monologue when a curtain suddenly ripped from its moorings. It narrowly missed Miss Hayes, but did manage to dump decades of dust and debris all over the cast. With true regal aplomb, Miss Hayes carried on without missing a beat.

FROM GRANDMOTHER'S COOKBOOK

Queen Cakes

One pound of flour, one of sugar, one of butter, eight eggs, one teacup of cream, a wine-glass of rose-water, and a pound of currants. Mix like pound-cake, leave out a tablespoonful of flour to mix through the currants, add them last, and bake in little tins.

In many ways Lula Naff got as much publicity as the stars she booked — in memoirs and even New York theatrical columns. In her autobiography, Katharine Cornell described Mrs. Naff as a town character who peddled tickets on the street from a shoe box, wearing a black sweater with the pockets stuffed with bananas and odds and ends of papers. The description amused Mrs. Naff, who said she never munched a banana on the street and never used a shoe box in her life — it was a shirt box. She was irritated, however, that Cornell spelled the name of her beloved auditorium "Rymer."

Bananas Cornell

This might have been a good way for Mrs. Naff to use any leftover bananas when a show closed.

½ cup packed brown sugar
¼ cup rum
¼ cup butter
2 large bananas
Vanilla ice cream
½ cup chopped walnuts

Combine the brown sugar and rum in a 1½-quart glass dish. Add the butter. Microwave on High for 4 to 5 minutes, stirring once. Cut the bananas into halves crosswise and lengthwise. Add to the syrup, turning to coat well. Microwave on High for 1 to 2 minutes. Serve hot over vanilla ice cream. Sprinkle with the walnuts.

Yield: 4 servings.

Poster courtesy of Nashville Room, Nashville and Davidson County Library

Garden Party Stuffed Baguette

Your guests will enjoy this appetizer, even if they miss the excitement of a Tallulah hose-down at your next garden party.

1 (24-inch) French bread baguette
8 ounces cream cheese, softened
2 tablespoons lemon juice
2 green onions, chopped
2 tablespoons chopped fresh dill, or
    1 teaspoon dillweed
1 (10-ounce) package frozen
    chopped spinach, thawed
4 cups minced cooked ham
½ cup chopped pecans
½ cup mayonnaise
1 tablespoon Dijon mustard

Cut the baguette into halves lengthwise and scoop out the centers, reserving ½-inch shells. Reserve the scooped-out bread for another use. Combine the cream cheese, lemon juice, green onions and dill in a bowl and mix well. Press the spinach to remove moisture. Add to the cream cheese mixture and mix well. Spread evenly over the insides of the bread shells.

Combine the ham, pecans, mayonnaise and mustard in a bowl and mix well. Spoon into the bread shells. Place the bread halves together and wrap tightly in plastic wrap. Chill for several hours. Slice to serve.

Yield: 20 servings.

The sultry Tallulah Bankhead appeared at the Ryman in both "Private Lives" and "Reflected Glory." Her appearances created as much fuel for gossip as for theatrical reviews, for she was known to gather reporters and admirers backstage, alternately charming and shocking them with her antics. After one appearance, however, when Bankhead was invited to a cocktail party at the home of a Nashville socialite, she became angered by what she decided was the deliberate upstaging by her hostess and turned the garden hose on the lady and her guests.

Poster courtesy of Nashville Room, Nashville and Davidson County Library

Brownies

This recipe was published in an interview with Katharine Hepburn years ago. She says that the secret is in the small amount of flour.

½ cup butter
½ cup baking cocoa
2 tablespoons vegetable oil
1 cup sugar
2 eggs
½ teaspoon vanilla extract
¼ cup flour
¼ teaspoon salt
1 cup chopped pecans
¼ cup butter, softened
½ cup baking cocoa
1 teaspoon vanilla extract
Salt to taste
2 cups confectioners' sugar
3 tablespoons milk

Katharine Hepburn

Melt ½ cup butter in a heavy saucepan; remove it from the heat. Stir in ½ cup baking cocoa, oil and sugar. Add the eggs and ½ teaspoon vanilla, mixing well. Stir in the flour, salt and pecans. Spoon into a greased 8x8-inch baking pan.

Bake at 325 degrees for 30 minutes. Cool on a wire rack. Cream ¼ cup butter in a mixer bowl until light. Add ½ cup baking cocoa, 1 teaspoon vanilla, salt, confectioners' sugar and milk; mix until smooth. Spread over the brownies. Cut into squares.

Yield: 16 servings.

Photograph courtesy of Nashville Room, Nashville and Davidson County Library

Katharine Hepburn appeared with Van Heflin and Joseph Cotten in "The Philadelphia Story" in 1941 and played to a standing-room-only house. Minnie Pearl has been quoted as saying that the performance was the most memorable of any non-Opry event she ever attended there.

Honey Popcorn

Invite your friends to enjoy an evening of old movies and serve this delicious treat.

> 1 cup honey
> 1 cup packed brown sugar
> 1 cup margarine
> 1 teaspoon salt
> ½ teaspoon baking soda
> 1 cup peanuts
> 5 quarts popped popcorn

Combine the honey, brown sugar, margarine and salt in a saucepan. Simmer for 2 minutes, stirring constantly. Remove from the heat and stir in the baking soda. Combine with the peanuts and popcorn in a large baking pan, tossing to coat well.

Bake at 250 degrees for 1 hour, stirring occasionally.

Yield: 20 cups.

Even the Ryman could not remain untouched by the growing popularity of the movies. In a few instances, the management actually unrolled a screen made from a thick muslin sheet and showed educational movies. More often than that, however, it was the stars whose names and faces had become famous on the silver screen that drew the audiences to see them on the stage. Jean Harlow, Greer Garson and Eve Arden all appeared at the Ryman. Charlie Chaplin, Mary Pickford, Douglas Fairbanks and Francis X. Bushman all lent their support to the war work of the Nashville branch of the American Red Cross.

Doris Day had yet to make "big-name" status when she appeared with Bob Hope and the Les Brown Band at the Ryman in 1949. The appearance broke all previous records for attendance and receipts at the Auditorium. Hope recounted the story that Captain Ryman had poured all his liquor into the Cumberland when he was converted and quipped that "Les Brown's Band heard about it and before we could stop them, they had on their diving trunks."

Sicilian Cheese Casserole

Doris Day, who supports the Doris Day Pet Foundation, has contributed this delicious meatless main dish.

1 medium eggplant
1 small onion, chopped
3 tablespoons olive oil
1 cup tiny shell pasta, cooked
3 ounces tomato sauce
¼ cup chopped parsley
2 tablespoons lemon juice
½ cup olive halves
Minced garlic to taste
½ teaspoon basil
½ teaspoon marjoram
Salt and pepper to taste
8 ounces Monterey Jack cheese, thinly sliced
1½ cups grated Parmesan cheese

Doris Day with Cary Grant

Peel the eggplant and cut it into ½-inch pieces. Sauté the eggplant and onion in the olive oil in a skillet. Combine with the pasta, tomato sauce, parsley, lemon juice, olives, garlic, basil, marjoram, salt and pepper in a bowl and mix lightly. Spoon into a 2-quart baking dish. Top with the cheeses.

Bake at 375 degrees for 30 minutes.

Yield: 6 servings.

Bob Hope, a star of radio's golden years, takes a turn behind the WSM microphone — one of radio's most famous microphones.

Favorite Chicken Hash

Bob Hope shared this recipe with Jimmy Carter when he worked with him on a Habitat for Humanity project.

2 chicken breasts, broiled
2 slices crisp-fried bacon, crumbled
½ small onion, chopped
Salt and pepper to taste
½ teaspoon lemon juice
2 tablespoons butter
1 teaspoon dry sherry
2 tablespoons sour cream

Cut the chicken into thin strips. Combine with the bacon, onion, salt, pepper, lemon juice and butter in a skillet. Cook until the onion is tender. Stir in the sherry and sour cream. Cook just until heated through. Serve immediately.

Yield: 2 servings.

When he appeared there in 1949, Bob Hope described the Ryman as "America's most picturesque institution" and an intimate old place, asking if he could have it when it fell down, but begging the management not to take off the Band-Aids until he had gotten out. Hope enjoyed having a sold-out house, saying, "But it was really a sellout and people were sitting on anything they could find. One woman complained when the manager gave her something to sit on. Halfway through the show she discovered it was her husband."

Movie fans had become
familiar with the Ryman
through such movies
as "W.W. and the Dixie
Dancekings" and "Honky
Tonk Man." Distinguished
movie director Robert
Altman, however, raised it
to new heights when he used
the Auditorium as a
metaphor for the city of
Nashville and for the country
as a whole in his movie
"Nashville." Since then, the
Ryman has been the
setting for Sissy Spacek's
re-creation of the role
of Loretta Lynn in
"Coal Miner's Daughter"
and Jessica Lange's
interpretation of Patsy Cline
in "Sweet Dreams."

Pan de Elote

Robert Altman's wife, Kathryn, serves this popular dish at parties. The name translates as "bread of corn", but the consistency is more pudding-like.

Robert Altman

> 1 (16-ounce) can cream-style corn
> 1 cup baking mix
> 1 egg, beaten
> 2 tablespoons melted butter
> ½ cup milk
> 1 (4-ounce) can chopped green chiles
> 8 ounces Monterey Jack cheese, thinly sliced

Combine the corn, baking mix, egg, butter and milk in a bowl and mix well. Spoon half the mixture into a greased 8x8-inch baking dish. Layer with the green chiles and cheese. Top with the remaining batter.

Bake at 400 degrees for 20 minutes or until golden brown.

Yield: 6 servings.

Cheese Crispies

Tere Myers never likes to eat a full meal before going on stage; she and Mandy enjoyed snacking on these before their performances in "Always... Patsy Cline." Being from Texas, she likes lots of cayenne, but recommends that you vary the amount of cayenne to suit your tastes.

    2 cups shredded Cheddar cheese
    2 cups flour
    1 cup melted margarine
    2 cups crisp rice cereal
    Garlic salt to taste
    Cayenne to taste

Combine the cheese, flour, margarine, cereal, garlic salt and cayenne in a bowl and mix by hand. Shape into ¾- to 1-inch balls and place on a greased baking sheet. Press with a fork dipped in hot water to flatten. Bake at 350 degrees for 15 minutes or until golden brown.

Yield: 4 dozen.

Tere Myers and Mandy Barnett in "Always...Patsy Cline"

Photograph courtesy of Ryman Archives

In recent years, the Ryman Auditorium has offered two original dramatic productions highlighting the lives of two of the most famous and beloved stars of the Grand Ole Opry. In 1994 and 1995, Mandy Barnett starred in "Always...Patsy Cline" based on the star's life. Tere Myers played Patsy's friend Louise Seger. In 1996, Jason Petty starred in "Lost Highway" based on the life of Hank Williams.

OPERA
HOUSE

...FROM GRAND OPERA TO GRAND OLE OPRY

Most people who connect the Ryman only with the Grand Ole Opry are surprised to find out that its stage was not built for Opry music at all. It was built for the opera.

In 1901, the New York's Metropolitan Opera came to Nashville — an unheard of occurrence in those days — to perform the somewhat risqué *Carmen*. The scene was a far cry from Sam Jones' tent revivals. Still, *Carmen* set a precedent which eventually lured many of the great stars of opera's Golden Age to the Ryman's stage, among them tenors Enrico Caruso and John McCormack.

But it wasn't opera that truly made the Ryman famous. It was Opry. In 1925, the Grand Ole Opry went on the air on new station WSM. Actually, it wasn't called the Opry at that time. It was the WSM Barn Dance until "The Solemn Old Judge," announcer George D. Hay, coined the name in 1927.

"For the past hour, we have been listening to music taken largely from Grand Opera," Hay told radio listeners. He was referring to the classical programming that preceded the barn dance.

"But from now on," Hay continued, "we will present 'The Grand Ole Opry.'"

The Opry played out of Studio B on the fifth floor of the National Life and Accident Insurance Company, which owned WSM. But the radio program quickly became such a hit that Studio B couldn't handle the audiences who came for the broadcast.

The Opry went in search of a more suitable home. After landing for a time at three different theaters around Nashville, all of which were soon outgrown, the Opry came to the Ryman. The exact date is something of a controversy. Some say it was 1941, some 1942, and some swear it was 1943. The most convincing proof points to June of 1943.

When the Opry moved into the auditorium, Minnie Pearl, Uncle Dave Macon, Bill Monroe, Ernest Tubb, Pee Wee King, Eddy Arnold, and, one of the Opry's newest stars, Roy Acuff, moved with it. Over the years, the Ryman would see dozens of major stars join the Opry ranks.

The Grand Ole Opry is as simple as sunshine. It has a universal appeal because it is based upon good will and with folk music expresses the heartbeat of a large percentage of Americans who labor for a living.

—George D. Hay

Production of the opera Cavalleria Rusticana *at the Ryman in 1927*
Photograph courtesy of F. Robinson Collection, Vanderbilt University Library

It is a beautiful, historic new old building that holds many memories for me, and I am sure, every other performer who has stood on the stage of what can truly be called the Mother Church of Country Music.

—Earl Scruggs

In the forties, there was Lester Flatt, comedian Rod Brasfield, Whitey Ford, Red Foley, Grandpa Jones, The Willis Brothers, Lonzo and Oscar, George Morgan, Little Jimmy Dickens, and, of course, Hank Williams. The warm June night that Williams made his debut on the Ryman stage has been called the biggest event in country music. Singing "Lovesick Blues," Williams brought the house down. Some say he was called back for six encores, and there would have been more had host Red Foley not calmed the crowd by promising that Williams would appear again on the Opry.

Uncle Dave Macon

The early fifties brought Hank Snow, Faron Young, The Carter Family with Chet Atkins as their guitarist, Kitty Wells, Webb Pierce, Jumpin' Bill Carlisle, Johnny Cash, Jimmy C. Newman, Stonewall Jackson, Ferlin Husky, Wilma Lee and Stoney Cooper, and Porter Wagoner who brought along Dolly Parton. The fifties closed out with Del Reeves, Skeeter Davis, Jan Howard, Archie Campbell, and George Hamilton IV.

Patsy Cline, Loretta Lynn, Hank Locklin, and Bill Anderson all joined the Opry in the early sixties.

By then, the old building had seen better days. Although still structurally sound, the wooden pews were worn and dull, as was most every other aspect of the aging hall. It was said that if you sat in the cheap seats beneath the balcony, you were likely to get a Coke leaking down on your head.

Things were so crowded backstage, performers often spilled out into the alley behind the Ryman. There, they could stroll right into the back door of Tootsie's Orchid Lounge for a beer or over to Linebaugh's for a

Photograph courtesy of Grand Ole Opry Archives

104

bite of dinner. Young Opry hopefuls hung out in the alleyway hoping to be discovered, and stars passed the time playing practical jokes on each other. Winos would stagger by and even an occasional lady of the evening would ply her trade. Lower Broadway hadn't seen such shenanigans since the days of Captain Tom Ryman's rowdy bunch.

Meanwhile, out in front of the building, the fans continued to line up by the thousands hoping to get a seat inside the Ryman. Often the line would begin forming in the early afternoon, people waiting for hours in the heat or cold to see the Grand Ole Opry.
If they were lucky enough to get inside, they would bring along ham sandwiches and fried chicken, and buy Cokes from the Ryman's concession stand. Since the building was not air conditioned, a hand fan was a must for Nashville's sticky summer evenings.

By 1964, the Grand Ole Opry's roster listed 55 star acts, 100 performers in all. Among those who joined about this time were Ernie Ashworth, Dottie West, Willie Nelson, and the Osborne Brothers. Tex Ritter, Bobby Bare, Ray Pillow, Stu Phillips, Jack Greene, Charlie Walker, Jeannie Seely, the Four Guys, and Dolly Parton rounded out the decade.

The Opry continued at the Ryman through the early seventies. Tom T. Hall, David Houston, Barbara Mandrell, Connie Smith, Jerry Clower, and Jeanne Pruett all joined before the Opry moved, Pruett being the last singing artist to join while it was still in the Ryman.

...the audience stamped their feet on the ol' Ryman's wooden floor with such wild enthusiasm that dust rolled up into the air, giving the air itself a strange, ethereal bluish hue that (I) would never forget.

—Grant Turner about Hank Williams' first performance at the Ryman

*The first star of grand opera
to appear at the Tabernacle
was Marcella Sembrich,
who had first appeared with
the Boston Festival
Orchestra. She returned with
the Metropolitan Opera
in 1901, for the only two
performances of that
250-person company ever
given in the city. A
new stage was built for
her performances as Rosina
in "The Barber of Seville."
"Faust" and "Carmen"
were also performed, with
some brows raised at the
appearance of that feisty
heroine of easy virtue on the
stage of the Tabernacle.*

Paczki

*This recipe for Polish Bismarcks would have
been familiar to the Polish belcanto soprano
Marcella Sembrich.*

*1 envelope dry yeast
1 cup (105- to 115-degree) milk
3½ cups flour
⅓ cup sugar
½ teaspoon salt
⅓ cup melted margarine or butter
2 eggs, slightly beaten
1 teaspoon vanilla extract
½ teaspoon grated orange peel
Vegetable oil for frying
Confectioners' sugar*

*Polish Soprano Marcella
Sembrich*

Dissolve the yeast in the warm milk. Mix the flour, sugar and salt in a
large bowl. Add the yeast mixture and margarine and mix well. Add
the eggs, vanilla and orange peel and mix to form a dough. Place in
a greased bowl, turning to coat the surface. Let rise, loosely covered,
in a warm place for 1 hour or until doubled in bulk. Toss lightly on a
floured surface until no longer sticky. Shape into 30 balls. Place on
a lightly floured tray. Let rise, covered, for 20 minutes.

Fry in 3 to 4 inches of hot oil in a skillet for 1 minute on each
side or until golden brown; drain. Sprinkle with confectioners' sugar
while warm.

Yield: 30 bismarcks.

Photograph courtesy of Metropolitan Opera Archives

Steak Bonne Femme

Emma Calvé's Great Dane would have had no complaints about this steak. If you don't fancy rare steak, cook it to your taste.

½ large red onion, thinly sliced into rings
10 medium mushrooms, sliced
½ clove of garlic, minced
1½ teaspoons butter
1½ teaspoons corn oil
2 (6-ounce) top sirloin steaks,
    ¾ inch thick
2 tablespoons beef broth
Salt and freshly ground pepper to taste

Metropolitan Opera Director Maurice Grau

Warm an ovenproof platter in a 200-degree oven. Sauté the onion, mushrooms and garlic in the butter and oil in a large skillet until tender. Increase the heat. Sauté until the onion is light brown and the juices have evaporated. Remove with a slotted spoon. Add the steaks and additional butter and oil if necessary to the skillet. Cook for 3 to 4 minutes on each side for rare. Remove to the warm platter.

Add the broth to the skillet, stirring to deglaze. Cook until the liquid is reduced to the desired consistency; reduce the heat. Add the onion mixture. Cook until heated through. Season with salt and pepper. Spoon over the steaks.

Yield: 2 servings.

Photograph courtesy of Metropolitan Opera Archives

Maurice Grau, director of the Metropolitan Opera on its national tour in 1901, had scheduled the great Emma Calvé in the title role in "Carmen" at the Union Gospel Tabernacle, but the famous singer failed to appear. Two local ladies were sent to inquire as to the nature of her indisposition. They discovered that she had worked herself into such a rage because the hotel had served her Great Dane well-done steak instead of rare that she was unable to sing. Fortunately for Nashville audiences, she recovered from this affront to return to sing at the Ryman in later years and was very popular with audiences.

In 1904, Madame Adelina Patti sang at the Tabernacle, performing not only the great operatic arias for which she was celebrated, but also a selection of popular sentimental tunes. Of course, she performed her famous rendition of "Home, Sweet Home." Unfortunately, a janitor chose a moment midway through her song to shovel coal into the two big stoves at the front of the Auditorium. The interruption disconcerted Madame Patti for only a moment; she overcame the noise by singing much louder.

Home Sweet Home-Style Biscuits

These may not have evoked home for the Spanish-born Madame Patti, but they certainly would for generations of audiences at the Ryman. To use this recipe for dumplings, omit the baking soda and shortening, roll the dough thin and cut it into strips. Cook in simmering chicken broth just until cooked through.

> 2 cups flour
> 1 teaspoon baking powder
> ¼ teaspoon baking soda
> 1 teaspoon salt
> ⅓ to ½ cup shortening
> 1½ cups buttermilk

Mix the flour, baking powder, baking soda and salt in a bowl. Cut in the shortening until crumbly. Stir in the buttermilk. Roll or pat on a floured surface. Cut with a biscuit cutter and place on a baking sheet.

Bake at 425 degrees for 12 to 15 minutes or until golden brown.

Yield: 1 dozen.

FROM GRANDMOTHER'S COOKBOOK

Beat Biscuit

One pint sweet milk, table-spoonful of lard, a little salt; use flour to make a very stiff dough; lay the dough on a strong pastry table, beat with a maul for 1/2 hour till the dough blisters and cracks; roll quite thin, cut out the biscuit, prick with a fork and bake in a moderate oven till well done.

Peach Melba

*The famous French chef Auguste Escoffier created this dish in honor of
Dame Nellie Melba.*

½ cup currant jelly
1 cup sieved raspberries
1 teaspoon cornstarch
½ cup sugar
Salt to taste
3 large peaches, peeled
1½ cups vanilla ice cream
Whipped cream

Mix the currant jelly and the raspberries in a double boiler. Stir in
the cornstarch, sugar and salt. Cook over boiling water until
thickened, stirring constantly. Chill until serving time. Combine
the peaches with water to cover in a saucepan. Cook until tender;
drain. Cut the peaches into halves, discarding the pits.

Chill until serving time. Place the peach halves cut side up on
serving plates. Fill with ice cream. Spoon the raspberry sauce over
the top. Top with whipped cream.

Yield: 6 servings.

*Opera was always a popular
drawing card at the Ryman.
Helen Porter Mitchell thrilled
Ryman audiences with her
coloratura soprano voice as
Dame Nellie Melba — the stage
name she took from her home
town of Melbourne, Australia,
and her 1918 decoration as
Dame Commander in the Order
of the British Empire. Her
performance was followed by
such performances as the return
of "Carmen" with the New
York Civic Opera, whose advance
publicity announced that the
program would take place at the
"Rymon" Auditorium.*

Chicken Cacciatore

This dish is popular in Caruso's native Naples, where it would be served with pasta, polenta or crusty Italian bread.

Lula Naff made the daring decision to book Enrico Caruso and Amelita Galli–Curci on consecutive nights at the Ryman in 1919. Galli–Curci had already been booked to present a program on April 30 when Mrs. Naff learned of the possibility of booking Caruso between engagements in Atlanta, where he was singing with the Metropolitan Opera, and St.Louis. The only night available, however, was April 29. The engagement was booked and the house was full for Caruso, who was one of the biggest box office draws of the period.

4 pounds cut-up chicken
1 large clove of garlic, minced
⅓ cup olive oil
2 cups chopped peeled tomatoes
1 large onion, sliced
1 large green bell pepper, chopped
1 rib celery, chopped
1 carrot, sliced
½ cup marsala
½ teaspoon oregano
1 teaspoon salt
¼ teaspoon freshly ground pepper
4 ounces mushrooms, sliced

Enrico Caruso in "La Gioconda"

Rinse the chicken and pat dry. Sauté with the garlic in the olive oil in a large skillet for 10 minutes or until evenly browned on all sides. Add the tomatoes, onion, green pepper, celery, carrot, wine, oregano, salt and pepper.

Simmer, covered, for 40 minutes, adding a small amount of water if necessary. Add the mushrooms. Cook for 15 minutes longer.

Yield: 6 servings.

Art courtesy of F. Robinson Collection, Vanderbilt University Library

Risotto alla Milanese

This dish is typical of Milan, where Amelita Galli-Curci was born and studied opera. You may vary the recipe by the addition of mushrooms or chicken livers.

> 1 onion, minced
> 6 tablespoons butter
> 2 cups uncooked rice
> ½ cup dry white wine
> 5 cups (about) boiling chicken bouillon
> ½ teaspoon ground saffron
> Salt and white pepper to taste
> ⅔ cup grated Parmesan cheese

Sauté the onion in the butter in a heavy saucepan until tender but not brown. Add the rice. Sauté for 3 to 4 minutes or just until transparent. Stir in the wine. Cook for 3 minutes. Add ½ cup of the bouillon. Cook until the bouillon is absorbed, stirring constantly. Add the remaining bouillon ½ cup at a time, continuing to cook and stir until the liquid is absorbed after each addition and stirring in the saffron, salt and pepper about halfway through the cooking time; cooking time will be about 20 to 25 minutes after the first addition of bouillon for rice al dente. Stir in the cheese.

Yield: 4 to 6 servings.

Because Galli-Curci's booking for her second visit to the Ryman had been arranged so far in advance, she actually drew a larger crowd than Caruso, who appeared on the preceding night. Her manager was flattered that the regular seats were sold out and chairs were sold on the stage. Mrs. Naff recalled that bouquets arrived by the dozens for the singer and she was given a great ovation in one of the greatest two-night programs of opera that opera lovers anywhere ever experienced.

Turkey Tetrazzini

Singer Luisa Tetrazzini was the inspiration for this well-known dish. It can be prepared with turkey or chicken.

½ cup flour
Nutmeg to taste
1½ teaspoons salt
½ cup melted butter or margarine
2 cups milk
1 (10-ounce) can chicken broth
2 egg yolks
½ cup half-and-half
¼ cup dry sherry
12 ounces thin spaghetti, cooked, drained
4 cups chopped cooked turkey
1 cup sliced mushrooms
¾ cup grated Parmesan cheese

Whisk the flour, nutmeg and salt into the melted butter in a large saucepan. Cook until bubbly. Stir in the milk and chicken broth. Cook for 2 minutes or until slightly thickened, stirring constantly. Beat the egg yolks with the half-and-half in a small bowl. Stir a small amount of the hot white sauce into the egg yolks; stir the egg yolks into the white sauce. Cook until heated through, stirring constantly; remove from the heat. Stir in the wine. Place the spaghetti in a 9x13-inch baking dish. Pour 2 cups of the white sauce over the spaghetti. Stir the turkey and mushrooms into the remaining sauce. Spoon over the spaghetti and sprinkle with the cheese. Bake, covered, at 350 degrees for 25 minutes. Bake, uncovered, for 10 minutes longer.

Yield: 8 servings.

Zarzuela de Mariscos

Interpreted literally as Musical Comedy of Shellfish, this dish is typical of the setting of Rossini's Spanish comic opera, "The Barber of Seville."

1 onion, chopped
¼ cup olive oil
2 cloves of garlic, minced
¼ cup chopped parsley
2 tablespoons tomato paste
1 pound small shrimp, peeled
1 pound lobster meat, chopped
½ cup dry white wine
Salt and pepper to taste
18 fresh clams
1 teaspoon ground saffron

Sauté the onion in the hot olive oil in a saucepan until golden brown. Add the garlic, parsley, tomato paste, shrimp and lobster. Pour the wine over the top and season with salt and pepper. Simmer, covered, for 10 minutes. Simmer the clams in water to cover in a saucepan until the shells open. Remove half of each shell and place the clams on the remaining half shell in the saucepan with the seafood mixture. Add the saffron. Simmer just until the seafood is cooked through. Ladle into soup bowls to serve.

The impresario Charles Wagner presented many famous operas at the Ryman, including "Madame Butterfly," and "La Boheme," as well as new versions of "The Barber of Seville" and "Faust." All boasted full orchestras and chorus, dazzling costumes and beautiful scenery; many also starred singers from the Metropolitan Opera. It is to be assumed that these were festive occasions at the Ryman, although it is a little hard to reconcile Lula Naff's report that at one such program, which the governor and his wife attended, "many of the ladies had on evening garb...that swept the peanut shells from the steps, as they paraded up and down."

Yield: 6 servings.

Poster courtesy of Nashville Room, Nashville and Davidson County Library

The Tennessean *reported that five thousand people were unable to get seats in the Ryman Auditorium when Nashville's own Ward–Belmont school presented "Cavalleria Rusticana" with local talent in 1927. A second performance had to be given the following night to accommodate the demand for tickets. The opera was staged by G.S. de Luca, teacher at Ward–Belmont and former teacher of several Metropolitan Opera stars. Members of the Nashville Symphony, conducted by F. Arthur Henkel, provided the music. A ballet was presented by Sara Jeter of Ward–Belmont during the intermission.*

Linguine alla Rustica

This Italian dish would have been appropriate to serve at parties after those festive performances of "Cavalleria Rusticana" in 1927.

8 ounces boned chicken
2 tablespoons olive oil
1½ teaspoons minced garlic
Basil, oregano, salt, black pepper and red pepper flakes to taste
1 tablespoon lemon juice
1 ounce pine nuts
12 medium shrimp, peeled
4 ounces sun-dried tomatoes, julienned
2 tablespoons butter
2 ounces mixed greens
2 tablespoons grated Parmesan cheese
1 (16-ounce) package angel hair pasta, cooked

Ward–Belmont's presentation of "Cavalleria Rusticana" at the Ryman with local talent in 1927

Rinse the chicken and pat dry; cut into strips. Heat the olive oil in a large sauté pan. Add the chicken and seasonings. Sauté until the chicken is light brown. Add the lemon juice, pine nuts, shrimp, tomatoes and butter. Cook over medium heat until the shrimp turn pink, stirring constantly. Add the greens, cheese and pasta, tossing to mix well. Serve immediately.

Yield: 4 servings.

Photograph courtesy of F. Robinson Collection, Vanderbilt University Library

Pasta e Fagioli

Relatives of Opry stage manager Vito Pellettieri recall his fondness for this bean and pasta dish, which is similar to one he prepared from a recipe he credited to his Italian grandfather, a Garibaldini.

1 cup dried white beans
Water
8 ounces cooked smoked ham, cut into small cubes
½ cup finely chopped onion
½ cup finely chopped celery
1 clove of garlic, minced
2 tablespoons olive oil
2 tablespoons chopped parsley
½ teaspoon rosemary
Salt and freshly ground pepper to taste
1 cup uncooked ditalini
Grated Parmesan cheese

Solemn old "Judge" George D. Hay

Sort and rinse the beans. Soak in 2 quarts of water in a large saucepan for 8 hours. Drain the beans, reserving the water. Add enough cold water to measure 2 quarts and return to the saucepan. Sauté the ham, onion, celery and garlic in the olive oil in a skillet for 10 minutes or until light brown. Add to the beans with the parsley, rosemary, salt and pepper. Bring to a boil and reduce the heat.

Simmer, partially covered, for 1½ hours or until the beans are tender. Remove half the beans with a slotted spoon and process in a food processor until smooth. Add to the soup with the pasta. Simmer for 10 to 15 minutes or until the pasta is tender. Adjust the seasonings. Ladle into soup bowls and top with the cheese.

Yield: 6 servings.

Photograph courtesy of Grand Ole Opry Archives

George D. Hay generally gets the credit for originating the "WSM Barn Dance" in 1929 and for changing its name to the Grand Ole Opry, although the Opry did not move into the Ryman Auditorium until 1943. The radio program followed the "Music Appreciation Hour" under the direction of the conductor and composer, Dr. Walter Damrosch. Hay announced that "For the past hour we have been listening to music taken largely from Grand Opera, from now on we will present The Grand Ole Opry" — a name that has stuck. It was Vito Pellettieri, the WSM music librarian, who became the first stage manager, a position that he held for forty years.

Dr. Humphrey Bate on the far left and the Possum Hunters: (left to right) fiddler Oscar Stone, banjoist Walter Liggett, guitarists Staley Walton and Paris Pond, and bass violinist Oscar Albright

Dr. Humphrey Bate's daughter claims that her father should have the credit for originating what became the Grand Ole Opry because Bate's group did the first Saturday night "barn dance" on WSM in 1925, several weeks before Judge Hay came. Bate had played the Ryman that same year for a policeman's benefit. Hay said of Bate, "Folk music was his hobby and he played a harmonica with considerable dexterity." It was he who named the group "The Possum Hunters," telling his musicians, back when Opry music was mostly instrumental, to "keep it close to the ground, boys," close to the simple truths of life.

Southern Garlic Grits

These would be good with possum if you know any modern-day possum hunters, but they are equally good at breakfast or as a side dish with any meat. Add some chopped jalapeños for extra zest if you find grits bland.

> 1 cup quick-cooking grits
> 4 cups boiling water
> ½ teaspoon salt
> 1½ cups shredded Cheddar cheese
> ½ cup butter
> ½ cup milk
> 2 eggs, beaten
> 1 clove of garlic, minced

Stir the grits into the boiling water in a heavy saucepan. Add the salt. Return to a boil and reduce the heat. Cook for 2½ to 5 minutes or until thickened, stirring occasionally. Stir in the cheese, butter, milk, eggs and garlic. Cook over low heat until the cheese melts. Spoon into a greased 2-quart baking dish. Bake at 350 degrees for 1 hour.

Yield: 6 servings.

Photograph courtesy of Grand Ole Opry Archives

Cool and Easy Lemon Pie

This recipe from the Martha White's Southern Sampler *cookbook, has a cookie-like crust that is made with Martha White Bran Muffin Mix.*

1 (7-ounce) package Martha White Bran Muffin Mix
1 cup chopped pecans
6 tablespoons melted butter or margarine
1 (14-ounce) can sweetened condensed milk
1 (6-ounce) can frozen lemonade concentrate, thawed
4 ounces whipped topping

Combine the muffin mix, pecans and butter in a mixer bowl and mix well. Crumble ½ cup of the mixture into a square baking pan. Press the remaining crust mixture over a 9-inch pie plate. Bake both the crust and the crumbled mixture at 350 degrees for 10 to 12 minutes or until light brown. Stir the crumbled mixture to break into fine crumbs. Cool on a wire rack.

Combine the condensed milk and lemonade concentrate in a mixer bowl and mix well. Fold in the whipped topping. Spoon into the cooled crust. Sprinkle the crumbs over the top. Chill for several hours before serving.

Yield: 6 to 8 servings.

A Message from our Sponsor

*Now you bake right (Ah ha) —
With Martha White (Yes, Ma'am).
Goodness gracious, good and light,
Martha White.
For the finest biscuits ever wuz —
Get Martha White Self–Rising Flour,
The one all–purpose flour,
Martha White Self–Rising Flour has got Hot Rize.*

There have been many well-known sponsors of the Grand Ole Opry, the first being Crazy Water Crystals, soon followed by LeGear's Animal Tonics, Pet Milk, Prince Albert Smoking Tobacco, Ralston Purina, Jefferson Salt, RC Cola, and others.

The longest continuing sponsor today, however, is Martha White, beginning in 1948 and entertaining with its famous Martha White bluegrass jingle written as a commercial in the early 1950s for just $100 by the late Pat Twitty of Nashville. The song was immortalized by Opry stars Earl Scruggs and Lester Flatt and is preserved on their album recorded in Carnegie Hall.

Grandpa Jones

Louis Marshall Jones, or Grandpa Jones, has been a "grandpa" longer than most people. He originated the character in 1935 at the age of twenty-two, and has since earned the grizzled mustache and wrinkles that used to be part of the costume. He is known for his role as a comedian, but he is also one of the world's finest traditional five-string banjo players. One of his memories of the Ryman dates back to his early Opry days on a night when Cowboy Copas was the master of ceremonies. "When I walked out on stage he said, 'Grandpa, where's your hat?' I paused a moment, rolled my eyes upward and asked, 'Ain't it up there?'"

Grandpa's Buttermilk Biscuits

Grandpa makes this recipe with oil, but he says that lard tastes better.

> 1½ tablespoons vegetable oil
> ¾ cup buttermilk
> 2 cups self-rising flour

Blend the oil and buttermilk in a bowl. Add the flour and mix to form a stiff dough. Knead lightly on a floured surface. Roll ½ inch thick and cut with a biscuit cutter or glass. Place in a greased baking pan. Bake at 400 degrees for 25 minutes or until evenly browned on top. May use all-purpose flour and add 1 teaspoon baking powder, ¼ teaspoon baking soda and ½ teaspoon salt if you prefer.

Yield: 1 dozen.

Photograph courtesy of Grand Ole Opry Archives

Peanut Butter Pie

Mae describes this recipe as a family "pass on down" dessert.

> 1 envelope unflavored gelatin
> 1 cup milk
> 1 cup sugar
> 4 eggs, separated
> ¼ teaspoon salt
> ½ to ¾ cup peanut butter
> 1 teaspoon vanilla extract
> ¼ cup sugar
> ½ cup whipping cream
> 1 baked (9-inch) pie shell
> 6 ounces semisweet chocolate
> ⅓ cup evaporated milk
> 1 cup confectioners' sugar
> ½ cup honey

Sprinkle the gelatin over the milk in a double boiler and let stand to soften. Heat over simmering water until the gelatin dissolves. Stir in 1 cup sugar, egg yolks and salt and mix until smooth. Cook until the mixture thickens enough to coat the back of the spoon, stirring constantly. Remove from the heat and beat in the peanut butter and vanilla. Chill until thickened. Beat the egg whites until frothy. Add ¼ cup sugar gradually, beating constantly until stiff peaks form. Beat the whipping cream until soft peaks form. Fold the egg whites and whipping cream into the chilled mixture. Spoon into the pie shell. Chill until firm. Combine the chocolate and evaporated milk in a saucepan. Cook over low heat until the chocolate melts, stirring to mix well. Add the confectioners' sugar and honey and beat until smooth. Spread over the chilled pie. Chill until serving time.

Yield: 8 servings.

Mae Boren Axton remembers sitting backstage at the Ryman in 1955 when she was asked for a song by Jack Stapp of Tree Publishing Company. She answered that she had a million seller named "Heartbreak Hotel" but had promised it to Elvis Presley. As Jack hurried to start the Prince Albert portion of the show, which he produced, he called, "I don't care who does it, just so I publish it." Mae answered, "You've got it," and the rest is history, although Mae gave Elvis one-third of the writer's rights, because during the months she came to know him and his family, she took pity on the fact that they were struggling financially at the time.

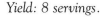

Country Ham and Eggs Casserole

This recipe is from Minnie Pearl Cooks, *the cookbook by Roy Acuff's great friend and fellow performer. As a native of East Tennessee, Roy appreciated good country ham.*

> 2 (10-ounce) cans cream of mushroom soup
> 1 soup can milk
> 1½ cups ground or finely chopped country ham
> 12 hard-cooked eggs, sliced
> 1 (4-ounce) can sliced mushrooms, drained
> ⅔ cup cracker crumbs

Combine the soup and milk in a bowl and mix well. Layer the ham, eggs, mushrooms and soup mixture ½ at a time in a greased 1½-quart baking dish. Top with the cracker crumbs. Bake at 350 degrees for 20 minutes.

Yield: 8 servings.

Vito Pellettieri with Roy Acuff

Roy Acuff was given the title "King of Country Music" by his longtime friend and baseball great Dizzy Dean and he is remembered as one of the best-loved performers ever to grace the stage of the Ryman. In an unsuccessful race for governor against his good friend Democrat Gordon Browning he defended the charge that he was a "hillbilly fiddler" rather than a serious candidate, saying, "I have no apologies for the kind of music I have been bringing to my people...It is the folk music of the South and...I am proud of it." Judge Hay said of Acuff, "His head and heart joined the fingers which handled his fiddle and bow and it was not long before he started to burn up the countryside like a forest fire."

"Good-Bye Turkey" Casserole

This recipe for leftover turkey is from Minnie Pearl Cooks, *in which Minnie says, "I never heerd of a casserole til I was a growed woman. We didn't have 'em in Grinders Switch, along with runnin' water, 'lectricity, sling pumps, and you name it. (We didn't have them neither.)"*

*Sarah Colley Cannon
as Minnie Pearl*

5 tablespoons flour
1 teaspoon salt
¼ teaspoon onion salt
¼ cup melted butter or margarine
2¼ cups milk or light cream
1⅓ cups uncooked quick-cooking rice
1½ cups turkey or chicken broth
½ cup shredded American cheese
1 (15-ounce) can asparagus spears, drained
2 cups sliced cooked turkey
2 tablespoons toasted slivered almonds

Blend the flour, salt and onion salt into the melted butter in a saucepan. Stir in the milk. Cook over low heat until thickened, stirring constantly. Place the rice in a greased shallow 2-quart baking dish. Pour the broth over the rice and sprinkle with half the cheese. Layer the asparagus and turkey over the rice. Spread the white sauce over the layers and sprinkle with the remaining cheese.

Bake at 375 degrees for 20 minutes. Top with the toasted almonds.

Yield: 6 servings.

Minnie Pearl's "How-dee! I'm just so proud to be here!" warmed the hearts of millions of appreciative fans, as did her stories about everyday happenings in Grinders Switch and her attempts to "ketch a feller." She remembered one of the first Opry performances at the Ryman: "You see, the stagehands changed those advertising flats back there and the rest of the people knew...not to come out on the stage until the scenery was changed. But I was so overeager, so avid, to get out there...that I ran out there before they got it changed and one of those sand bags came down and hit me." When asked if it knocked her out, she replied, "Well, it didn't help me any."

Calzones

*Russell Faxon, sculptor from
Bell Buckle, Tennessee, created
the "Oh, Roy!" sculpture
of Roy Acuff and Minnie Pearl,
in the renovated Ryman
Auditorium, to express the
fifty-year friendship
between the two. He relates,
however, that he must have
been chosen for his artistic skill
rather than his vast
knowledge of country music
history. "After touring the
Ryman, I imagined the two
sitting on a bench backstage.
One of my designs had Roy
playing and singing to a
starry-eyed Minnie. The chief
project designer, Mike
Summers, placed a sympathetic
hand on my shoulder
and said, 'Russ, Roy never
played the guitar!'"*

5¾ to 6¼ cups flour
1 envelope dry yeast
⅓ cup dry milk powder
¼ cup sugar
1 teaspoon salt
2 egg whites
¼ cup melted light margarine
1¼ cups very warm water
1 pound ground beef
2 or 3 cloves of garlic, crushed
½ cup each chopped onion and mushrooms
12 to 18 ounces tomato sauce or red Italian sauce
Italian seasoning, salt and pepper to taste
½ cup shredded mozzarella cheese
¼ to ½ cup grated Parmesan cheese

*Russ Faxon with his sculpture of
Minnie Pearl and Roy Acuff*

Combine 1½ cups flour with the next 7 ingredients in a large bowl and beat for 2 to 3 minutes. Stir in the remaining flour. Place in an oiled bowl, turning to coat the top. Let rise, covered, for 1½ to 2 hours or until doubled in bulk. Brown the ground beef in a skillet, stirring until crumbly; drain. Add the garlic, onion and mushrooms. Sauté until the onion is tender. Add the tomato sauce, Italian seasoning, salt and pepper. Simmer until reduced to the desired consistency. Divide the dough into 2 portions. Roll each portion ⅛ inch thick on a floured surface. Cut into 4-inch squares. Place a rounded tablespoon of the ground beef mixture on each square and sprinkle with the cheeses. Fold the dough to enclose the filling, moistening the edges to seal well. Place seam side down on oiled baking sheets. Let rise for 30 minutes. Bake at 350 degrees for 15 to 20 minutes or until golden brown.

Yield: 12 to 24 small calzones.

Chili

This recipe is one used by the family of President Lyndon Johnson at their Pedernales River ranch. Chili meat in Texas is coarsely ground or finely chopped round steak or trimmed chuck.

4 pounds chili meat
1 large onion, chopped
2 cloves of garlic, minced
1 teaspoon oregano
1 teaspoon comino seeds
2 tablespoons (or more) chili powder
1½ cups canned tomatoes
Pepper sauce and salt to taste
2 cups hot water

Brown the chili meat lightly with the onion and garlic in a large heavy saucepan. Add the oregano, comino seeds, chili powder, tomatoes, pepper sauce, salt and hot water. Bring to a boil and reduce the heat. Simmer for 1 hour, skimming the fat as necessary.

Yield: 12 servings.

FROM GRANDMOTHER'S COOKBOOK

Son of a Gun Stew

Take the heart, liver, brains, melt, sweet bread, marrowgut and a small portion of fat and lean scraps of meat out from the head and put in a small amount of water in a pot and cook this slowly for 3 or 4 hours. Season with salt and pepper and sometimes a little chili powder. It this was too soupy, thicken with flour. Keep a lid on tight and cook slowly. Eat this with sour dough biscuits.

Singing cowboys were popular at the Ryman, beginning with Bob Wills and his Texas Playboys and their version of "San Antonio Rose." They were followed by the Golden West Cowboys, the Sons of the Pioneers, and Ernest Tubb with his Texas Troubadours. Roy Rogers brought his horse Trigger on stage for his performance — an accompaniment that has not been repeated by a singer. Gene Autry, who sang at the Ryman, also claims the distinction of singing, in military uniform, at the Texas performance at which Dizzy Dean introduced Roy Acuff as the "King of Country Music."

Applesauce Cake

Tennessee Ernie, a longtime spokesperson for Martha White, credits this recipe to Mama Ford. It appears in the Martha White Southern Sampler *cookbook.*

3 cups boiling water
1 (16-ounce) package raisins
5 cups sifted Martha White flour
1 teaspoon baking powder
2 teaspoons baking soda
1 tablespoon cinnamon
1 teaspoon cloves
½ teaspoon salt
1 cup butter or margarine, softened
3 cups packed light brown sugar
2 cups applesauce
1 cup chopped black walnuts

Tennessee Ernie Ford

Pour the boiling water over the raisins in a medium bowl and let stand for several minutes. Sift the flour, baking powder, baking soda, cinnamon, cloves and salt together. Cream the butter in a large mixer bowl until fluffy. Add the brown sugar and applesauce and beat until smooth and light. Add the dry ingredients gradually, mixing until smooth after each addition. Drain the raisins and stir into the batter with the walnuts. Spoon into a greased and floured 10-inch tube pan.

Bake at 325 degrees for 1¾ hours or until a wooden pick inserted 1 inch from the edge comes out clean. Flavor improves if the cake is allowed to stand for several days before serving.

Yield: 12 to 15 servings.

Singer and spinner of homespun humor Tennessee Ernie Ford sang at the Opry many times and once filled in for Red Foley on the Prince Albert segment. Ford's wife was expecting their first child after seven years of marriage when he was invited for his first appearance at the Ryman. Unable to refuse the invitation to sing on the Opry, he came without her and learned when he arrived that the baby had been born. He passed out cigars from the stage of the Ryman that night and was so excited about the combined birth and Opry debut that he couldn't remember what he sang. Minnie Pearl always remembered that he sang "Anticipation Blues."

Sour Cream Coconut Cake

Kitty found this an easy cake to make during her busy career as a country music star and homemaker.

12 ounces frozen coconut, thawed
8 ounces sour cream
1 cup sugar
1 teaspoon vanilla extract
1 (2-layer) package yellow butter cake mix
2 cups whipping cream
¼ cup confectioners' sugar, sifted
½ teaspoon vanilla extract
8 ounces frozen coconut, thawed
¼ cup sugar

Combine 12 ounces coconut, sour cream, 1 cup sugar and 1 teaspoon vanilla in a bowl and mix well; set aside. Prepare and bake the cake mix using the directions for 3 layers. Cool in the pans for several minutes; remove to wire racks to cool completely. Stack the layers on a serving plate, spreading the coconut mixture between the layers.

Beat the whipping cream with the confectioners' sugar and ½ teaspoon vanilla in a mixer bowl until soft peaks form. Spread over the top and side of the cake. Mix 8 ounces coconut and ¼ cup sugar in a bowl. Sprinkle over the top and side of the cake, pressing in gently. Store in the refrigerator until serving time.

Yield: 16 servings.

Kitty Wells

Kitty Wells blazed a trail for female singers at the Opry in 1952 with a song whose lyrics about a trusting wife gone wrong were at first questioned by many as inappropriate for the stage. Kitty had "retired" from what seemed like an unpromising career in country music when the song "It Wasn't God Who Made Honkey-Tonk Angels" was offered to her along with a chance to sing it on the Opry. The song was written in response to the Hank Thompson hit "The Wild Side of Life." She remembers her first appearance as "an awesome, inspiring time to stand where so many great artists...had performed."

Hank Snow is recognized for his years as an Opry member by Hal Durham, former Opry announcer, general manager and current Grand Ole Opry and Opryland Productions Group President.

Hank Snow's first memory of the Ryman was a painful one. After a very checkered career, his song "Brand On My Heart" became the number one song in Texas and he was invited to sing it on the Opry in 1950. Recalling the experience he said, "I don't mind telling you that I bombed. The people just sat there while I sang. No applause, no nothing, almost. Just sat." On the way home that night he told his wife that he was never going back there again, and he might not have if his next song, "I'm Movin' On," hadn't been such a hit that it received the ultimate compliment — a parody by Jethro Burns of Homer and Jethro —and established his career.

Pineapple Casserole

Hank and Min Snow like to serve this tasty side dish.

> 2 cups sugar
> 3 eggs, beaten
> ½ cup milk or cream
> ½ cup melted butter
> 4 cups bread cubes, crusts trimmed
> 1 (20-ounce) can juice-pack pineapple chunks

Combine the sugar, eggs, milk and butter in a bowl and mix well. Stir in the bread cubes and undrained pineapple. Spoon into a baking dish. Bake at 350 degrees for 45 to 60 minutes or until bubbly.

Yield: 8 servings.

Photograph courtesy of Grand Ole Opry Archives

Cajun Deer Roast

Jimmy Newman shares this recipe from his days growing up in Big Mamou, Louisiana.

1 venison roast
2 cloves of garlic, sliced
Salt and pepper to taste
Thick-sliced bacon
1 cup water

Cut slits in the roast and place the garlic slices in the slits. Sprinkle generously with salt and pepper. Place in an oiled roasting pan. Cover with the bacon. Add the water to the pan.

Roast, covered, at 350 degrees for 1 to 1½ hours. Roast, uncovered, until tender, basting every 20 to 30 minutes. Serve the pan drippings over rice.

Yield: varies, depending on the size of the roast.

Rachel Veach and Velma Williams preparing backstage at the Ryman for their appearance with Roy Acuff's band

Jimmy C. Newman was a Cajun from Louisiana, but he didn't sing Cajun music. He sang country music with a French accent and had trouble getting a chance to do it until his own composition "Cry, Cry, Darling," won him a chance to sing on the Opry. He remembers that he couldn't afford the loud costumes with embroidery and rhinestones that were popular when he came to the Ryman in the fifties. Two occasions that stand out in his mind include his first performance there as a guest of George Morgan, who was hosting the show, and the time when he met his idol Gene Autry backstage at the Auditorium.

Photograph courtesy of Grand Ole Opry Archives

Hank Williams' performance at the Ryman Auditorium made a lasting mark on country music history.

One of the most memorable events at the Ryman was Hank Williams' first appearance there and the record of it comes to us from Grant Turner as he told it to Hank's daughter Jett. Grant introduced Hank that night to sing his hit song "Lovesick Blues." The audience was lukewarm, never having seen Hank before. But as soon as Hank began singing, the audience went wild and "stamped their feet on the ol' Ryman's wooden floor with such wild enthusiasm that dust rolled up into the air, giving the air itself a strange, ethereal bluish hue that Grant said he would never forget. He never saw it happen before, and he never saw it after that night, nor will any of the rest of us."

Stuffed Chicken Breasts

Hank Williams' daughter Jett likes to prepare this easy chicken recipe.

8 chicken breast halves, skinned, boned
8 thin slices ham
8 slices Swiss cheese
1 envelope brown gravy mix
1 (10-ounce) can cream of mushroom soup
½ cup chicken stock

Rinse the chicken and pat dry. Pound flat with a meat mallet. Layer 1 slice of ham and 1 slice of cheese on each piece of chicken. Roll to enclose the ham and cheese and secure with a skewer. Place in a baking dish. Combine the gravy mix, soup and chicken stock in a bowl and mix well. Pour over the chicken.

Bake at 325 degrees for 1 hour.

Yield: 8 servings.

Long-time Grand Ole Opry announcer Grant Turner witnessed the career beginnings of a host of country music legends.

Rancho Delight Corn Bread

Grant Turner's recipe from the Martha White Southern Sampler cookbook reflects his early days in Texas.

    1 egg
    ¾ cup milk
    1 (6½-ounce) package Martha White Mexican Cornbread Mix
    2 sausage patties, cooked, chopped
    ⅔ cup crushed corn chips

Beat the egg in a bowl. Add the milk and cornbread mix; stir until smooth. Stir in the sausage and corn chips. Pour into a greased 8-inch cast-iron skillet or baking pan.

Bake at 425 degrees for 15 to 18 minutes or until golden brown.

Yield: 6 servings.

One of the real keepers of the Ryman's memories was Grant Turner. Turner came from Abilene to Nashville's WSM in 1944, where he was taken under the wing of Judge George D. Hay, who assigned him to the half-hour portion of the Opry sponsored by Crazy Water Crystals. His tenure on the Grand Ole Opry was to carry him through the Opry days at the Ryman to the move to the new Opry House, and to earn him the name of the dean of country music announcers and a place in the Country Music Hall of Fame.

Chet Atkins began appearing at the Ryman in 1946, working the "Sunday Down South" shows as well, and went on to exert a monumental influence in country music. As a guitarist, he has developed picking styles that are essential studies for any would-be guitar virtuoso and that have won him 13 Grammy Awards and a place in the Country Music Hall of Fame. He took part in the Ryman's 1996 Tennessee Bicentennial Concert with Steve Wariner, Larry Carlton and Leo Kottke. He still, however, remembers hanging out at the stage door in the old days watching Robert Lunn, "The Talking Blues Man," "audition" the hopefuls who crowded around the stage door, asking them to sing and dance on top of the old privy.

Sunday Down South Barbecued Spareribs

Sunday in the South still features such regional specialties as barbecued spareribs, served with corn light bread, baked beans, coleslaw and chess pie.

12 pounds spareribs
1½ tablespoons dry mustard
1½ tablespoons water
2 cups tomato pureé
1 cup vinegar
½ cup corn oil
½ cup packed light brown sugar
½ cup minced onion
1 teaspoon minced garlic
1 tablespoon salt, or to taste

Chet Atkins appeared on a number of radio shows when he first came to Nashville, including "Sunday Down South" at the Ryman.

Place the spareribs in a large roasting pan. Roast at 375 degrees for 1½ hours; drain.

Blend the dry mustard with the water in a saucepan and let stand for 10 minutes. Add the tomato pureé, vinegar, oil, brown sugar, onion, garlic and salt. Simmer for 10 minutes.

Spoon over the spareribs. Bake for 30 minutes longer.

Yield: 12 servings.

Saturday Night Apple Pie

This is the pie that Bill Carlisle looked for after a Saturday night performance at the Ryman.

> 6 cups sliced tart apples
> ½ to ¾ cup sugar
> ¾ teaspoon cinnamon
> ½ teaspoon nutmeg
> 1 recipe (2-crust) pie pastry
> 2 tablespoons butter

Combine the apples, sugar, cinnamon and nutmeg in a bowl and toss lightly. Place in a pastry-lined pie plate and dot with the butter. Top with the remaining pastry, seal the edges and cut vents.

Bake at 425 degrees for 50 to 60 minutes or until the apples are tender and the pastry is golden brown. May cover the edge with foil if necessary to prevent overbrowning.

Yield: 8 servings.

Bill Carlisle's most treasured memories of the Ryman are from the sixties, when his daughter Sheila and son Billy joined the group and they worked as a family. He says that after the Saturday night show Sheila would take a friend home and "they would open up cans of tomato soup, throw in some margarine and think they had created the gourmet meal of the century. I would 'pass' on the soup and go looking in the refrigerator for a slice of apple pie! My wife Leona and I would drift into a happy sleep as the kids picked and wrote and sang songs out in the den. We lost our daughter Sheila, but we've never lost the memories and there's not a time I see the Ryman that I don't give thanks for those blessed days."

Crowds waiting in line at the Ryman for tickets to the Opry

Photograph courtesy of Les Leverett

It was stage manager Vito Pellettieri who gave Jan Howard some good advice when she was first appearing as a guest on the Opry, advising her to stick to her own songs and plug her own records. Jan took his advice and made so many appearances on the Opry in the following years that most people assumed she was a member, but she did not actually join the roster until 1971.

Artichoke Frittata

Jan Howard enjoys cooking special recipes like this one for her friends. This can be cut into small squares for an appetizer, or large squares for a brunch or meatless main dish.

1 (12-ounce) jar marinated artichoke hearts
4 eggs, beaten
8 ounces small curd cottage cheese
1 small onion, minced
Rosemary, thyme, basil and marjoram to taste

Drain the artichokes, reserving 2 tablespoons of the marinade. Chop the artichokes and combine with the reserved marinade, eggs, cottage cheese, onion and seasonings in a bowl and mix well. Pour into a greased 8x8-inch baking dish.

Bake for 30 minutes or until light brown. Cut into squares.

Yield: 16 appetizer squares or 6 main dish servings.

Hank Locklin, Jan Howard, Tex Ritter and June Carter

Photograph courtesy of Grand Ole Opry Archives

Few stars stands out more than the unforgettable Patsy Cline, whose life was the subject of both the motion picture "Sweet Dreams" and an original musical production, "Always...Patsy Cline," at the Ryman. Jan Howard shares this memory of her first meeting with Patsy: Because Jan was very shy, Johnny Cash had advised her to just do her spot on the Opry and leave. She followed his advice, only stretching her stay out a bit if she had the chance to see her idol, Patsy Cline. "One night, after (Patsy) had been on, I was changing clothes in the ladies restroom/dressing room when the door flew open and there stood Patsy Cline. She stood there in her fringed skirt, boots and cowgirl hat with her hands on her hips and glared at me. I didn't say a word. 'Well,' she said, 'you're a conceited little S.O.B. You just waltz in here, do your spot and leave. You don't say hello, kiss my foot or anything else to anyone. Who do you think you are anyway?' I was crushed, but my Irish and Indian temper surfaced. Walking over to her, and with my hands on my hips, I said, 'Now wait just a darned minute! Where I was raised it was the people who live in a town that make a newcomer feel welcome. And not a darned soul has made me feel welcome here!' It didn't occur to me that my being afraid to introduce myself to anyone, thinking they would say, 'Jan who?' or 'So what' hadn't given anyone a chance to welcome me. Patsy stood there for a minute, then threw her head back and laughed a laugh that seemed to come from the soles of her feet. I just stood there dumbfounded. 'You're alright, honey,' she said. 'Anyone that'll talk back to the Cline is alright. We're gonna be good friends.' And from that moment on, we were. Patsy taught me something that night. If you expect to have friends, you have to be one."

The legendary Patsy Cline performing on the Opry at the Ryman

Photograph courtesy of Les Leverett

Family-Style Chicken Pie

This is one of the dishes Wilma Lee likes to cook for her family.

⅓ cup flour
1 teaspoon dry mustard
½ teaspoon salt
¼ cup melted butter
3 cups milk
3 cups chopped cooked chicken
1 (16-ounce) package frozen soup vegetables
1 cup shredded Cheddar or Swiss cheese
1 all ready pie pastry, cut into strips
1 egg yolk
1 tablespoon water

Blend the dry ingredients and butter in a saucepan. Cook until bubbly, stirring constantly. Stir in the milk gradually. Cook until thickened, stirring constantly. Add the chicken and vegetables. Simmer for 5 to 8 minutes. Stir in the cheese until melted. Spoon into a 9x13-inch baking dish. Arrange the pastry over the top in a lattice design. Brush with a mixture of egg yolk and water. Bake at 425 degrees for 15 minutes or until golden brown.

Yield: 8 servings.

FROM GRANDMOTHER'S COOKBOOK

Chicken Pie

*Take a nice fat hen, parboil until tender, remove all bones and shred
fine, then put back in the rich broth with a small piece of butter and black
pepper, then thicken with flour and sweetmilk; have a pan lined with a
rich crust made of milk and baking powder, as biscuit, pour chicken mixture
into pan and cover with a crust 1/4 inch thick with a small bit of butter
spread on top; bake until a light brown and serve hot.*

Tom T. Hall was recommended to Opry management by Ernest Tubb who described him as "a young guy...singing odd kinda songs."

Hot Water Corn Bread

This old southern favorite is also one of Tom T. Hall's favorites.

Cornmeal
Salt to taste
Hot water
Ice cubes
Vegetable oil for deep-frying

Combine the cornmeal with the salt in a bowl and stir in enough hot water to make a dough which can be kneaded. Rub hands with ice cubes to keep the dough from sticking and knead until smooth. Shape into egg-size balls. Deep-fry in hot oil until golden brown.

Yield: *variable.*

Tom T. Hall has written and sung some of the most moving lyrics ever enjoyed at the Opry. Of the Ryman Tom says, "When I was a young man learning to play the guitar, I loved the smell of the instrument. When a guitar is first taken from its case, the wood smell is like no other in the world. When I first walked into the Ryman Auditorium some thirty-five years ago, I was surprised to find the same smell. The polished wooden pews sat glistening in the afternoon sun that filtered through the windows and gave the aroma of a thousand old guitars. There's nothing else like it. It makes you hungry for good music."

Dixie Hall tells a story about the night Mother Maybelle received an award at the Ryman. Music City News, for which Dixie was writing at the time, decided to give the first of its presentations to Maybelle, the "Mother of Country Music," and the Ryman was selected as the venue. The manager, Ott Devine, gave his blessing, but turned down Dixie's request that Johnny Cash make the presentation, because John's unpredictable behavior had resulted in his being "out of favor" at the time. Hank Snow, a family friend, was suggested as the substitute. Hank agreed, if she would have Johnny standing by in case he "got tied up in traffic." Dixie told Maybelle that she was to present an award to Hank and asked her to wear her long black dress. She was kept busy in the wings, wondering how she could make the award if Hank were not there, while a tuxedo-clad "man in black" paced restlessly, with no sign of Hank. "Then," Dixie says, "it was time and someone handed the award to me saying, 'Go do it.' I heard the announcer saying 'Music City News Special Award' and then I was at the footlights. Looking down at the front row I saw John's former manager, Bob Neal, who gave me the thumbs-up sign. Right away then it became clear what I should do, and praying 'Forgive me, Mr. Devine,' I introduced 'the one and only Johnny Cash.' The Auditorium lit up with camera flashes as, in his own magnetic fashion, John strode out on stage, followed by the Carter sisters carrying long-stemmed red roses. The applause was deafening as the audience rose to its feet. Mr. Devine never mentioned the matter and that, friends, was the very first Music City News Award.

Johnny Cash in an early appearance on the Prince Albert portion of the Opry

Photograph courtesy of Grand Ole Opry Archives

Opry announcer Grant Turner, June Carter, and Archie Campbell on stage at the Ryman

Potato Candy

This is Mother Maybelle's own recipe for candy.

1 medium to large potato
1 (1-pound) package confectioners' sugar
Peanut butter

Boil the potato in the jacket in water to cover in a saucepan until tender; drain. Peel and mash the potato in a bowl. Add the confectioner' sugar and mix to form a stiff mixture. Roll into a rectangle on a work surface sprinkled with additional confectioners' sugar. Spread with peanut butter. Roll into a log to enclose the peanut butter; wrap with waxed paper. Chill until firm. Slice to serve.

Yield: 24 servings.

Mother Maybelle Carter was the matriarch of a singing family, made up of her daughters Helen, June and Anita, which joined the Opry in 1950 as the Carter Family, with Chet Atkins as their fiddler. June later caught the eye of a rising young star named Johnny Cash and they married. Of Johnny's debut, the Nashville Banner reported, "The haunting words of 'I Walk the Line' began to swell through the building. And a veritable tornado of applause rolled back. The boy had struck home, where the heart is... As his last words filtered into the farthermost corners, many in the crowd were on their feet, cheering, waving and clapping. They, too, had taken a new member into the family."

Photograph courtesy of Grand Ole Opry Archives

Southern-Style Barbecued Soybeans

*Skeeter Davis' grandfather used to grow soybeans, and, as a vegetarian,
she knows how valuable and nutritious they are in her diet. She hopes that
you will try this recipe.*

3 medium onions,
   chopped
2 tablespoons canola oil
1 (15-ounce) can stewed
   tomatoes, crushed
3 tablespoons tomato paste
2 cups water
1 tablespoon molasses
½ cup packed brown sugar
2 tablespoons soy sauce
½ cup vinegar
½ teaspoon allspice
1 teaspoon salt
4 cups cooked soybeans
Freshly ground pepper
to taste

*Skeeter Davis is pictured here with Dolly
Parton reminiscing about the Ryman
during the taping of her variety show in
1988. With Dolly are (left to right) Del
Wood, Jan Howard, Skeeter, Minnie Pearl,
Jeanne Pruett, Norma Jean and Jean
Shepard. Kitty Wells, although not shown,
was also present.*

Sauté the onions in the hot canola oil in a large non-aluminum
saucepan until tender. Add the tomatoes, tomato paste, water,
molasses, brown sugar, soy sauce, vinegar, allspice and salt and mix
well. Simmer for 4 minutes. Add the soybeans. Simmer, covered,
for 1½ hours or until thickened to the desired consistency, adding
additional water if needed. Season with pepper.

Yield: 8 servings.

Photograph courtesy of Donnie Beauchamp

"Big Iron" Skillet Potato Cakes

This recipe reminds us of Marty Robbins' 1960 hit "Big Iron" and of his boyhood Depression days in Arizona, when leftover potatoes would have always been served again.

2 cups leftover mashed potatoes
1 egg, beaten
2 tablespoons flour
1 tablespoon corn syrup
Salt to taste
2 tablespoons flour
¼ cup butter

Combine the potatoes, egg, 2 tablespoons flour, corn syrup and salt in a bowl and mix well. Shape into oval patties. Coat with 2 tablespoons flour and pat to ½-inch thickness. Fry in the butter in a cast-iron skillet over low heat until brown on both sides.

Yield: 6 servings.

Marty Robbins left his roistering days in Phoenix to become a successful singer, songwriter, businessman, and race car driver. He always wanted to host the late night, or 11:30, portion of the Opry, because that way he could spend the early part of the evening racing at the Nashville Speedway. Marty always put his fans first and that late portion had a tendency to stretch beyond the time limit, much to the chagrin of the Willis Brothers, who had to wait around until all hours to do the sponsor spots for Lava Soap. The problem was finally solved when the jingles for the late show were put on tape.

Marty Robbins

Roy Drusky's focus on recording country and southern gospel albums is related to his interest in strengthening family ties and encouraging young people. It ties in with his favorite memories of the Ryman, which he says are from the days when the Opry was performed there. "It was a 'family gathering' at that time and all of the artists were very close. I guess one of the fondest memories of all would be of sitting backstage with my wife and Stringbean and his wife Estelle, just talking, being together and sharing some very special moments in time."

Vita Burger Stew

Roy Drusky gets the TVB Vita Burger at the health food store and says to get the chunk style rather than the granules. He likes to cook this stew in the pressure cooker for 30 minutes, but gives us the method for preparing it on top of the stove.

2 cups TVB chunk-style Vita Burger
2 cups chopped onions
1 tablespoon vegetable oil
1½ cups sliced celery
2 cups sliced carrots
1 can tomatoes
3½ cups water
1 tablespoon McKay's
    beef seasoning
1 bay leaf
1 teaspoon salt
6 cups chopped potatoes
1 (8-ounce) can tomato sauce
1 (16-ounce) can peas, drained

David "Stringbean" Akeman

Soak the Vita Burger in water in a bowl overnight. Sauté the onions in the oil in a saucepan until tender. Drain the Vita Burger. Add to the saucepan with the celery, carrots, tomatoes, water, beef seasoning, bay leaf and salt. Simmer for several minutes. Add the potatoes. Cook until all the vegetables are tender. Stir in the tomato sauce and peas. Cook until heated through. Thicken with 2 tablespoons flour if needed for the desired consistency. Discard the bay leaf.

Yield: 8 servings.

Strawberry Bread

Sharon White Skaggs' recipe for strawberry bread freezes well.

- 1½ cups flour
- 1½ cups sugar
- ½ teaspoon baking soda
- ¼ teaspoon cinnamon
- ¼ teaspoon salt
- 1 cup crushed strawberries
- ¾ cup vegetable oil
- 2 eggs, beaten
- 1 cup chopped pecans

Mix the flour, sugar, baking soda, cinnamon and salt in a large bowl. Add the strawberries, oil, eggs and pecans and mix well. Spoon into a greased and floured large loaf pan. Bake at 350 degrees for 1 hour or until the loaf tests done. Remove to a wire rack to cool.

Yield: 1 loaf.

FROM GRANDMOTHER'S COOKBOOK

Sally Lunn

Three eggs, whites and yolks beaten separately, one quart of milk, a quarter of a pound of butter, two tablespoonsful of homemade yeast (more, if it is baker's) a tablespoon heaping full of sugar, flour enough to form a stiff batter, and a little salt. Warm the butter and milk together. When milk-warm, add the yeast, then the yolks of the eggs, then the flour, and last the whites; mix well together, and let it stand to rise four or five hours; then beat it up, pour it into the pan or Turk's head, and bake three-quarters of an hour. Serve hot.

Buck White drove his family 850 miles from Texas to go to the Opry in 1957, and waited in a line that "went all the way down to the corner, around the corner and way down Broadway." After the show they went outside and met Bill Monroe. As performers, however, The Whites didn't make the cut on their first try. They auditioned before Roy Acuff on the stage at the Ryman for the opening season of the Opryland Theme Park but failed to get the job. Their career brought them back to the Opry in 1984, however, when Roy Acuff introduced them as new members.

The Grand Ole Opry cast at the Ryman

One particular memory of performing at the Ryman stands out in Whisperin' Bill Anderson's mind. It took place on a hot summer night with the windows all open in the nonair–conditioned Auditorium, "with all kinds of little creatures coming and going. I was standing on stage singing and as I took a deep breath, a bug flew down my throat. I was standing up there going 'ahhh' trying to keep on singing but unable to get my throat cleared. One of Ernest Tubb's band members was standing behind me and he asked, 'What's the matter?' I turned around and choked out that a bug had flown down my throat. 'Well,' he said, 'then let the bug sing.'"

Shoofly Pie

Bill Anderson shares this version of one of his favorite old-fashioned desserts with us.

½ cup water
½ cup blackstrap molasses
½ teaspoon baking soda
1 cup sifted flour
1 cup packed brown sugar
1 teaspoon cinnamon
¼ cup butter, softened
1 (9-inch) pie shell, baked, cooled

Combine the water, molasses and baking soda in a bowl and mix well. Mix the flour, brown sugar and cinnamon in a bowl. Add the butter and mix until crumbly. Pour half the molasses mixture into the pie shell. Sprinkle with half the crumb mixture. Repeat the layers. Place on a baking sheet.

Bake at 350 degrees for 25 minutes or until set.

Yield: 6 to 8 servings.

Easy Pasta

Anyone can prepare and enjoy Jack Greene's easy pasta recipe. He serves it with good homemade bread.

> 1 package (¼-inch wide) green pasta
> 1 (1½x4-inch) piece mozzarella, bleu or feta cheese, shredded or
>   crumbled
> Italian salad dressing to taste

Cook the pasta using the package directions; drain. Toss the hot pasta with the cheese and salad dressing in a bowl. Serve immediately.

Yield: 6 servings.

Jack Greene being introduced by Ernest Tubb, his longtime friend and associate, for his Opry debut

Jack Greene dominated the Country Music Awards in 1967, the year he became a member of the Grand Ole Opry and went from being a drummer with Ernest Tubb to being the top male vocalist of the year. His memories include some firsts: "To me personally, the Ryman is where I first saw Roy Acuff, Patsy Cline, Jim Reeves, Marty Robbins, and the list goes on. It is the first place I worked with Ernest Tubb and was my introduction to the family of the Grand Ole Opry that I'm so proud to be a part of." Of the Ryman, Jack says, "She was built for the purpose of saving people from lost lives, yet she was destined to become the Mother Church of Country Music."

Photograph courtesy of the Ryman Archives

Part of the appeal of the Opry is that the music and the musicians alike come from the down-to-earth side of life. As Stonewall Jackson puts it, "I do hope that people understand that I'm a very grateful person. I came from humble beginnings, sharecropping down in South Georgia, and the business has been like a fairy tale to me." The fairy tale brought Stonewall to Nashville on a Wednesday in 1956 just to sell a song to Acuff Rose. That set in motion a chain of events that led to a Thursday audition for Judge Hay at the Opry, a performance on Friday night on the Opry Frolics and an appearance with Ernest Tubb's band at the Opry on Saturday night!

Special Meat Loaf

Stonewall Jackson says that he also pours a can of Creole sauce over this meat loaf just before it comes out of the oven.

> 1½ pounds ground chuck
> ½ cup chopped onion
> 2 tablespoons chopped green bell pepper (optional)
> 1 cup cracker crumbs
> 1 (8-ounce) can tomato sauce
> 1 medium bay leaf, crushed (optional)
> Marjoram, thyme and salt to taste

Combine the ground chuck, onion, green pepper, cracker crumbs, tomato sauce, bay leaf, marjoram, thyme and salt in a bowl and mix well. Pack into a loaf pan. Bake at 350 degrees for 1 hour or until cooked through.

Yield: 6 servings.

FROM GRANDMOTHER'S COOKBOOK

Hog's Head Cheese

Take a hog's head, have it nicely cleaned, cover with water, boil until very tender. Chop very fine, add salt, pepper, cloves and allspice; pour the liquor it was boiled in over it, return to the fire; stir frequently until it thickens; skim off the fat that rises to the top. When very thick pour in molds; let it stand all night, then turn it out bottom upwards. If well done it will be a beautiful jelly.

Picadillo

Justin Tubb says that this recipe is good served with beans, guacamole and tortillas. It can be used for empanadas, tacos and stuffed green peppers.

½ cup raisins
¼ cup water
2 pounds lean ground beef
3 tablespoons olive oil
1 large onion, finely chopped
1 clove of garlic, finely chopped
3 medium tomatoes, peeled, chopped
2 tart cooking apples, peeled, chopped
½ cup pimento-stuffed olives, cut
    crosswise into halves
2 or 3 jalapeños, seeded, chopped
½ teaspoon oregano
½ teaspoon thyme
Salt and pepper to taste
½ cup slivered almonds
1 tablespoon margarine
Cooked rice

Young Justin Tubb

Soak the raisins in the water in a bowl for 10 minutes. Brown the ground beef in the olive oil in a large heavy skillet, stirring until crumbly. Add the onion and garlic. Sauté until the onion is tender; drain. Stir in the tomatoes, apples, undrained raisins, olives, peppers, oregano, thyme, salt and pepper. Simmer for 20 minutes, stirring occasionally. Sauté the almonds in the margarine in a small skillet until golden brown. Spoon the beef mixture into the center of a large platter. Sprinkle with the almonds. Spoon the rice around the edge.

Yield: 6 to 8 servings.

Justin Tubb was just nine years old when he made his first appearance at the Ryman as a special guest of his father, Ernest Tubb, on the Opry. He still has a copy of Minnie Pearl's "Grinder's Switch Gazette" with a listing of his appearance on the schedule on the back cover. He became a regular member of the Grand Ole Opry in his own right at the age of twenty in 1955, on the Prince Albert portion hosted by George Morgan. At the time, he was the youngest male vocalist ever to become a member and the only "second generation" member, a record that stood until George Morgan's daughter Lorrie became a member in 1984.

Pat Boone's memories of the Ryman go back a long way, beginning with watching Red Foley do the Prince Albert portion of the Opry, while standing backstage with Red's daughter Shirley, with whom Pat says he was, and still is, madly in love. Later, he was asked to sing "Golden Rocket" at the Opry. "However, once I was backstage and realizing I was going in front of Hank (Snow's) audience on Hank's portion of the Opry, I had second thoughts. Why should I sing his song in front of his audience? So I asked Hank to please sing with me, and to take turns on the verses of that great classic of his, and he agreed. Thank God! What a treasured and priceless memory."

Golden Rockets

Pat says that these are a big favorite at the Boone house.

⅓ cup melted butter or shortening
1 cup packed brown sugar
1 egg, slightly beaten
1 teaspoon vanilla extract
1 cup flour
½ teaspoon baking powder
⅛ teaspoon baking soda
½ cup chopped nuts
½ package chocolate chips

Combine the butter and brown sugar in a mixer bowl and mix well. Beat in the egg and vanilla. Sift together the flour, baking powder and baking soda. Add to the brown sugar mixture gradually, mixing well after each addition. Stir in the nuts. Spread in a greased 9x13-inch baking pan. Sprinkle with the chocolate chips. Bake at 350 degrees for 25 to 30 minutes or until golden brown. Cool on a wire rack. Cut into squares.

Yield: 4 dozen.

Architects used glass fragments and researched many historical sources to restore the Auditorium's arched pediment window, which had been boarded up for twenty years.

Photograph courtesy of Donnie Beauchamp

Jeannie Seely

Cranberry Salad

Jeannie Seely's cranberry salad is a perfect addition to a holiday menu.

> 1 (6-ounce) package sugar-free strawberry gelatin
> 1 cup boiling water
> 1 (16-ounce) can whole cranberry sauce
> ½ cup cold water
> 1 (8-ounce) can crushed pineapple
> 1 apple, chopped
> ½ cup finely chopped celery
> ½ cup chopped walnuts

Dissolve the gelatin in the boiling water in a bowl. Stir in the cranberry sauce. Add the cold water, undrained pineapple, apple, celery and walnuts and mix well. Spoon into a mold. Chill until partially set. Stir to mix well. Chill until set. Unmold to serve.

Yield: 8 servings.

Jeannie Seely remembers the night, as a new cast member at the Opry, she really felt accepted. She was sharing the very small ladies' dressing room, in awe of "all these ladies that until recently I had only seen across the footlights from the audience. Jean Shepard, one of my absolute heroes, was trying to style her hair and getting a little frustrated. Suddenly she whirled around, shoved a comb and brush into my hands and said, 'Here, Seely, you ain't doing nothing, you do this — you can fix hair can't you, and hurry up, I'm about on!' I was thrilled and scared to death, but I smiled because I had a feeling I had just become 'one of 'em.'"

Dolly Parton

Many musical programs have been taped for television in the Auditorium. Dolly Parton, also a star of the Grand Ole Opry, returned to the Ryman to tape a part of a special for her ABC variety show there in 1988. She invited a group of "country women" to sit with her on that well-worn stage and reminisce about performances under its spotlights. Dolly's own early memories of the Ryman were as a child listening to the Opry on an old battery radio up in the foothills of the Smoky Mountains. Her first trip there was in 1956 at the age of ten, when she saw such greats as Hank Williams, and later Patsy Cline and Johnny Cash.

Beefy Cowboy Beans

Dolly says that you can substitute two cans of pork and beans for the fresh October beans in this recipe if you like.

    1 pound ground beef
    2 medium onions, finely chopped
    1 small green bell pepper, finely chopped
    4 cups cooked fresh October beans
    2 cups catsup
    1 teaspoon vinegar
    ¼ cup packed brown sugar
    1 teaspoon mustard
    1 teaspoon salt
    1 teaspoon pepper

Brown the ground beef with the onions and green pepper in a 10-inch skillet, stirring until the ground beef is crumbly; drain. Add the October beans, catsup, vinegar, brown sugar, mustard, salt and pepper and mix well. Spoon into a baking dish.

Bake at 350 degrees for 15 to 20 minutes or until bubbly.

Yield: 8 servings.

Fresh Orange Juice Cake

Caterer TomKats served this cake when Dolly Parton was taping her television series from the Ryman for ABC. Dolly was very calorie conscious at the time and was assured that it was very low-fat, probably no more than 2,000 calories a bite, but worth every bite.

> 4 eggs
> ½ cup vegetable oil
> 1 cup fresh orange juice
> 1 (2-layer) package yellow cake mix
> 1 package instant coconut pudding mix
> 1 cup sugar
> ½ cup butter
> ½ cup fresh orange juice

Combine the eggs, oil and 1 cup orange juice in a mixer bowl and mix until smooth. Add the cake mix and pudding mix and beat for 2 minutes at medium speed. Spoon into a greased and floured bundt pan. Bake at 350 degrees for 40 minutes. Combine the sugar, butter and ½ cup orange juice in a saucepan. Bring to a boil. Pour over the hot cake in the pan. Let stand for 5 minutes. Remove to a serving plate to cool completely.

Yield: 16 servings.

George Jones and Tammy Wynette at the Ryman in 1969

Photograph courtesy of Donnie Beauchamp

George Jones' first record was "There Ain't No Money In This Deal," and George says there wasn't, in fact, but he went on to a very successful career, joining the Opry in 1973. He tells us that "The first time I walked on stage at the Ryman, to me, was like being on top of the highest mountain in the world. It was the top, and yet at the same time I felt very humble standing there where so many of my heroes had stood before me. It occurred to me that their's were big shoes to fill and I felt uncertain. Then as I started in to singing I felt the warmth and the love that emanates from this grand ole building and I felt reassured, knowing this would always be home. This was the rock."

Dottie West

Shelly West tells us that her mother Dottie was always happiest when she was entertaining, whether it was singing or cooking for friends, or, sometimes, both. When the program "Lifestyles of the Rich and Famous" invited her to be a guest on their show, she shared some of her specially prepared munchies for the crew. Shelly says that "It was as if she could bring the sunshine right into her home," and she is remembered as the girl who was raised on country sunshine and happy with the simple things.

Texas Crabgrass

Shelly West has shared this recipe of her mom's — one she liked to serve to guests.

> 1 onion, chopped
> ½ cup butter
> 1 ounce crab meat
> 1 (10-ounce) package frozen spinach, thawed, drained
> ¾ cup grated Parmesan cheese
> 1 (4-ounce) can chopped green chiles
> Garlic salt to taste

Sauté the onion in the butter in a skillet. Add the crab meat, spinach, cheese, chiles and garlic salt and mix well. Simmer until heated through. Serve with chips as a dip.

Yield: 6 servings.

Oatmeal Refrigerator Cookies

*Steve and his two sons, Ross and Ryan, actually make these cookies and
have a lot of fun doing it. Although they do the kitchen cleanup afterward,
Steve admits that his wife Caryn does come in behind them "to remove
flour from the ceiling and other odd places." He gives credit for the recipe
to Country Fair Cookbook.*

1 cup shortening
1 cup sugar
1 cup packed brown sugar
2 eggs
2 teaspoons vanilla extract
1½ cups sifted flour
1 teaspoon baking soda
½ teaspoon salt
3 cups quick-cooking oats

Cream the shortening, sugar and brown sugar in a mixer bowl until
light and fluffy. Beat in the eggs 1 at a time. Blend in the vanilla. Sift
the flour, baking soda and salt together. Add to the creamed mixture
gradually, mixing well after each addition. Stir in the oats. Divide
the dough into 3 portions. Shape each portion into 1¼x10-inch rolls
and wrap in plastic wrap. Chill for several hours. Cut into thin slices
and place 1½ inches apart on ungreased baking sheets.

Bake at 400 degrees for 6 to 8 minutes or until light brown. Remove
to a wire rack to cool completely.

Yield: 8 dozen.

*Steve Wariner was just
seventeen when he first played
the Ryman, as backup for
Dottie West. As he tells it,
"Dottie and I were heading
downtown in her Cadillac, but
as usual, she was running
late. We pulled up to the Opry's
famous backstage door
when the announcer on WSM
said, 'Ladies and Gentlemen...
here she is from McMinnville,
Tennessee...' I'm seventeen
years old, I've never been in the
building...I'm freaking out...
I'm running past Marty Robbins
and Ernest Tubb, had no
idea where I was going, where
to plug in...I mean, I was
freaked out! Later that night, it
dawned on me: I just played
the Grand Ole Opry!"*

Black Bean Salsa

Try Barbara's black bean salsa as a dip with tortilla chips or as an accompaniment to Southwest menus.

1 (15-ounce) can black beans
1 medium tomato, seeded, chopped
Kernels of 2 ears of corn
½ small red onion, chopped
1 orange, peeled, chopped
1 small green bell pepper, chopped
1 small red bell pepper, chopped
2 teaspoons chopped cilantro
1 teaspoon minced jalapeño
3 tablespoons olive oil
1 tablespoon fresh lime juice
½ cup spicy vegetable juice cocktail
½ teaspoon garlic powder
Salt and pepper to taste

Barbara Mandrell on guitar,
Jerry Reed, Ronnie Shaw, Jimmy
Riddle, Onie Wheeler

Rinse and drain the beans. Combine with the tomato, corn, onion, orange, bell peppers, cilantro and jalapeño in a large bowl. Add the olive oil, lime juice, vegetable juice cocktail, garlic powder, salt and pepper and mix well. Chill until serving time.

Yield: 8 servings.

Barbara Mandrell had given up an early musical career to become a serviceman's wife. She decided to come out of "retirement" at the age of not quite nineteen, while on a visit to the Ryman. She was attending the Opry with her family, sitting in the balcony of the Auditorium, when she decided that this was what she wanted. "I decided I want this. I don't want to retire. So...I said to my father, 'If you'll manage me, I want to pursue this.' That's the moment in time, boom, that it happened, that I embarked on (my career)."

Photograph courtesy of Les Leverett

Great Hors d'Oeuvre

Joe Diffie says that even he can prepare this quick and easy appetizer and guests always enjoy it.

    1 (8-ounce) block cream cheese
    1 bottle cocktail sauce
    Crab meat
    Crackers

Place the cream cheese on a serving plate. Spoon the cocktail sauce over the cream cheese and top with the crab meat. Arrange your favorite crackers around the edge.

Yield: 8 servings.

Joe Diffie reports that one of the best memories he has of the Ryman was "hanging out backstage in the dressing room with Carl Perkins and the Lonesome Cowboy Band, listening to them swap stories. It was a great night, filled with old memories and ghosts of the past."

FROM GRANDMOTHER'S COOKBOOK

Grandmother's Cookbook never included any recipes for hors d' oeuvres and Minnie Pearl explained why in her cookbook, Minnie Pearl Cooks. She wrote, "We never had no cause for appetizers when I was a youngun. We wuz always hungry anyways. Specially Brother. He'd eat anything what wasn't nailed down tight."

*Tanya Tucker had the
opportunity to perform at the
Ryman on the last Friday night
that the Opry played there.
In her words, "I was backstage,
just hanging out, visiting and
privately paying my respects...
Jan Howard insisted on giving
up her spot on the show for me
and I was stunned...I remember
saying 'I can't do this, I'm just
wearing jeans.' The next thing I
knew, I was being carried on
stage by Jerry Clower! I think
I sang 'Delta Dawn.' I
don't really remember because
I was so overwhelmed by
the whole experience. I do know
that my heart was full of love
for Jan and Jerry and the
rest of the Opry family. I was
so proud to be there."*

Texas Lasagna

*Tanya makes this with her own salsa and says that you can use either
the mild or the hot. Top it with sour cream, fresh cilantro, black olives and
chopped red onions when it comes out of the oven.*

> 1 pound ground turkey
> 1 envelope taco seasoning mix
> ½ cup chopped onion
> 1 (28-ounce) can Tanya Tucker's Salsa, strained
> Cooked lasagna noodles
> 2 cups shredded nonfat Cheddar cheese
> 2 cups shredded nonfat mozzarella cheese
> 16 ounces nonfat cottage cheese

Brown the ground turkey in a skillet, stirring until crumbly. Add the
taco seasoning mix and onion. Cook until the onion is tender; drain.
Add the salsa. Simmer for 35 minutes. Reserve a small amount of
the Cheddar cheese and mozzarella cheese for the topping. Alternate
layers of meat sauce, noodles, the remaining Cheddar cheese, the
remaining mozzarella cheese and cottage cheese in a baking dish until
all the ingredients are used, ending with the reserved Cheddar and
mozzarella cheeses. Bake at 350 degrees for 45 minutes.

Yield: 6 servings.

*Renovations
at the Ryman*

Photograph courtesy of Ryman Archives

Mexican Caviar

LaCosta serves this recipe from her native Arizona with hot corn chips.

4 (14-ounce) cans black-eyed peas, drained
4 medium tomatoes, chopped
2 jalapeños, seeded, chopped
1 cup chopped parsley
2 (14-ounce) cans Shoe Peg corn, drained
8 to 10 green onions, chopped
1 cup chopped onion
2 medium green bell peppers, chopped
4 cloves of garlic, minced
1 (16-ounce) bottle Italian salad dressing

Combine the peas, tomatoes, jalapeños, parsley, corn, green onions, onion, green peppers and garlic in a large bowl. Add the Italian salad dressing and mix well. Chill for 2 hours or longer. Drain before serving.

Yield: 20 servings.

FROM GRANDMOTHER'S COOKBOOK

Hot Tamales

3 lbs. choice beef, 1 lb. pork boiled tender, 6 pods choice pepper, (remove seed and boil until soft) 2 pods garlic, 1/4 teaspoon camenie seed, Mexican sage, 1 teaspoon black pepper, 2 of salt, 1 cup lard. Grind all together. 1/2 gallon meal, 1 teaspoon salt, 1 cup lard, mix with cold water to thickness of paste, spread heaping teaspoon on shuck, then put on ground meat, roll, put in dinner pot and cover with cold water; cook 45 minutes over slow fire. To prepare shucks cut ends off and scald.

Wilma Lee and Stoney Cooper introduced LaCosta Tucker when she first appeared at the Ryman. As she sang, she says that she remembered the many nights that she and her sister had listened to the Opry growing up in Arizona. "And to think that now I was standing there and in the wings I could look over and see Tex Ritter and Ernest Tubb and Minnie Pearl and I could only know in my heart that my dream had finally come true and just maybe some other little girl was out there, dreaming just as I had about singing at the Ryman in Nashville, Tennessee. What a glorious night!"

TOWN
HALL

...THE VOICE OF AMERICA

As one of Nashville's principal gathering places, the Ryman always served as much more than just a place of entertainment. Even in its earliest days, political rallies were held there — something that occasionally got Captain Tom Ryman in hot water.

Important political figures and lecturers visited there through the years, as well as famous figures espousing a variety of causes. Important conventions were held — it was the massive Confederate Veterans Association's reunion in 1897 that effectively built the balcony — as well as revivals, school graduations, wrestling matches, and even livestock shows. It was, and still is, a Town Hall in the truest sense, evidenced by the prestigious gathering of Secretaries of Defense to discuss the situation in Bosnia in 1995.

In the earliest years, Commodore Matthew Perry, perennial presidential candidate William Jennings Bryan, and Booker T. Washington came to speak. In 1907, President Theodore Roosevelt gave a rousing address at the Ryman. Eleanor Roosevelt later spoke from the same stage on behalf of the Girl Scouts, and Helen Keller appeared with teacher Anne Sullivan Macy.

The tone hasn't always been serious, however. Among the "speakers" were W.C. Fields and Will Rogers, both of whom espoused their wonderful humor here. Nationally beloved weatherman Willard Scott has made several visits here, and Garrison Keillor has broadcasted his down-home "Prairie Home Companion" radio show from the renovated Ryman several times.

In fact, Keillor's radio show was the first public event in the "new" Ryman, an appropriate debut for the hall. As some two million people listened in on 278 stations across the country, Keillor recalled the first time he'd been there, looking in through open windows in the summer of 1974, and the last time, when the Opry last played there.

Of course, there is no longer a need for open windows. A modern heating and cooling system was part of the Gaylord restoration, a project that had construction workers putting in ten- to twelve-hour

The music drifted out — high lonesome voices about being left behind, walked out on, dropped, shunned, shut out, abandoned, and otherwise mistreated...
—Garrison Keillor

Eleanor Roosevelt with Girl Scout Council officials during her visit to the Ryman in 1933
Photograph courtesy of Girl Scout Council of Cumberland Valley

*It is a sign of a
good civilization for
cities to preserve
and maintain historic
areas such as the
Ryman Auditorium.
—Caspar Weinberger*

days, six and seven days a week to open on schedule. The sound
system, lighting, and staging facilities had all been brought up to modern standards. A ticket sales area, bathrooms, offices, retail space, dressing rooms, and TV production facilities were added.

Although the new additions and accommodations were well
received, what impressed visitors and performers most was how much of
the "old" Ryman remained. It was Gaylord's mission from the start to
keep as much of the original character as possible, inside and out, while
making the Ryman state-of-the-art. That was no easy feat, but one
accomplished with remarkable success.

Credit goes to the restoration plan's careful attention to the smallest
detail. For example, the old wooden pews — 250 of them — were
entrusted to an Alabama firm for refurbishing. The chewing gum was to
be scraped off and the finish restored, but the nicks and dings of time
were to be left intact.

The end result was a masterpiece. Amazingly, the Ryman
retained all its old feel, the acoustics were still incredible, the intimacy
between performer and audience was as good as ever. And now, many
remarked, it was air conditioned!

Those who were lucky enough to be included in the first
entertainment event there — the taping of the television special "The
Roots of Country: Nashville Celebrates the Ryman" — were astounded
at this phoenix that had risen from the ashes of time and neglect to
once again be a vital and vibrant hall.

Now, on any given week, the townspeople gather once again in
Captain Tom Ryman's auditorium. More often than not, music is a part
of that gathering, just as it was so many years ago.

The Ryman has embarked on a new era, one that will bring much
joy and inspiration to many lives in the years to come. If the history to
be written of this renaissance is only half as colorful as
that of the Ryman's original incarnation, Nashville is in for a treat.

And one can't help thinking that somewhere, somehow, Captain
Tom Ryman is smiling over it all.

The Confederate Gallery of the Ryman Auditorium

Barbecued Leg of Pork

The Confederate Veterans probably consumed a lot of barbecue at the convention held in Nashville. This wouldn't have made enough to serve them all, but it will serve a large crowd at your next party or family reunion. It is best prepared with a rotisserie. The sauce can be used with any cut of meat.

1 cup packed brown sugar
2 tablespoons flour
¼ cup (or more) vinegar
1 teaspoon dry mustard
¼ teaspoon ground cloves
1 (9- to 11-pound) boned and rolled leg of pork

Prepare the coals in a grill in advance and let them burn down to red and glowing ash. Combine the brown sugar, flour, vinegar, dry mustard and cloves in a bowl and mix well. Place the pork leg on the grill or on a rotisserie over the coals. Roast for 3 to 3½ hours or until close to 170 degrees on a meat thermometer. Brush with the sauce. Grill for 30 minutes longer, brushing frequently with the sauce.

Yield: 25 servings.

Photograph courtesy of Donnie Beauchamp

The Tabernacle was called on early in its history to serve the larger community. In June of 1897, it served as the headquarters for the reunion of 100,000 Confederate Veterans, one of many conventions held to coincide with the Tennessee Centennial Exposition. Sam Jones and Captain Tom Ryman spearheaded the project to build the gallery called for in the original plans and to name it The Confederate Gallery in honor of the event — a name it still carries today. Sam Jones gave an impromptu benefit to raise funds to pay the Louisville Bridge Company, the Indiana Church Furnishing Company and J.H. Yeaman for their work.

The Union Gospel Tabernacle's sacred status was the center of controversy during the fall of 1894 when both political parties held their gubernatorial conventions there. The press reported that the Tabernacle's supporters, most of whom were Republicans, were in favor of a third political party, "Tabernacleism." When Tom Ryman unwisely stated that the "Tabernacle Ticket" would probably win, his "gang" was lambasted by Joseph Dillin from the pulpit of the Tabernacle itself as a "rag-tag, bob-tail, whop-it-up-together-and-throw-it-in-a-bag-ticket." The incident so embarrassed Ryman that he decreed there would be no more politics from the Tabernacle's pulpit, but his ruling proved to be short lived.

Whop-It-Up-Together-and-Throw-It-in-a-Bag-Meal

This ticket is sure to win on your next camping trip or children's sleep-over party.

2 pounds round steak
2 onions, chopped
6 carrots, chopped
3 potatoes, chopped
1 (4-ounce) can sliced mushrooms
1 (10-ounce) can cream of mushroom soup
½ soup can water
Salt and pepper to taste

Cut the steak into 1-inch pieces. Combine steak with the onions, carrots, potatoes and mushrooms in a bowl. Add the soup, water, salt and pepper and mix well. Let stand for 10 minutes or longer. Spoon the mixture onto six 18-inch foil squares and fold the foil to seal well. Grill, covered, over low heat for 15 minutes on each side or until the steak and vegetables are tender.

Yield: 6 servings.

Chicken à la President

Roosevelt must have met many chicken dishes on his campaign and speaking tours, but he might have asked for seconds of this old favorite.

½ cup sliced mushrooms
3 tablespoons butter
3 tablespoons flour
1½ cups chicken stock or milk
1 egg yolk, beaten
1 cup chopped cooked chicken
¼ cup chopped pimento
Salt and pepper to taste
1 tablespoon dry sherry
¼ cup slivered almonds
¼ cup green peas
4 patty shells

The Vanderbilt football team that greeted Theodore Roosevelt

Sauté the mushrooms in the butter in a saucepan. Sprinkle with the flour. Cook until bubbly, stirring constantly. Add the chicken stock. Cook until thickened, stirring constantly. Stir a small amount of the sauce into the egg yolk; stir the egg yolk into the sauce. Cook until slightly thickened. Add the chicken, pimento, salt and pepper. Stir in the sherry, almonds and peas. Cook just until heated through. Serve in the patty shells.

Yield: 4 servings.

The most famous political figure to appear at the Ryman was President Theodore Roosevelt, who spoke of reform and economic prosperity there in 1907. The whole city mounted a grand celebration with a 21-gun salute fired from Capitol Hill. Preparations included plans for keeping boisterous Vanderbilt students from disrupting the proceedings, but when the President complimented Vanderbilt's football team, he was interrupted so often with cries of "Bully" from the students that he spoke longer than planned. He later visited the campuses of Peabody and Vanderbilt, where he was greeted with the cheer: Rah, rah, rah, rah, rah, rah, Teddy Bear, Teddy Bear, Boo-oo-oo-oo.

League of Nations Ground Beef Patties

America's all-time favorite, the hamburger, can be modified to give it the international flavor of your choice. Just add any of the following choices to one pound of ground beef, shape it into patties and grill or broil to your taste.

All-American Choices
 2 teaspoons prepared mustard
 Chopped chives or onions
 2 tablespoons pickle relish
 ½ envelope onion soup mix
 3 tablespoons barbecue sauce
 Bacon, crisp-fried and crumbled
 Shredded cheese

South American Choices
 ½ envelope taco seasoning mix
 1½ tablespoons chopped green chiles
 2 teaspoons chili powder
 3 tablespoons chili sauce

Asian Choices
 2 tablespoons soy sauce
 5 teaspoons teriyaki sauce
 3 tablespoons chopped water chestnuts

Italian Choices
 2 tablespoons grated Parmesan cheese
 Italian seasoning
 Chopped olives
 1 tablespoon chopped basil

French Choices
 2 tablespoons crumbled bleu cheese
 2 tablespoons shredded Gruyère cheese
 3 tablespoons chopped scallions

Woodrow Wilson's proposed League of Nations stirred a great deal of national debate and the Ryman was the scene of one of those. United States Senators W.E. Borah, Henry Cabot Lodge, Jim Reed, Robert L. Owen, Carter Glass, Frank O. London and Hiram Johnson met on the Ryman stage shortly after World War I to debate the issue before a crowd of interested spectators.

All-American Apple Pie

*Bryan's support of national
values was as down-to-earth
as this apple pie.*

½ cup golden raisins
½ cup chopped walnuts
⅔ cup packed brown sugar
1 tablespoon flour
½ teaspoon grated
     lemon peel
½ teaspoon cinnamon
¼ teaspoon mace
Salt to taste
5 or 6 apples, peeled,
     thinly sliced
1 recipe 2-crust pie pastry
2 tablespoons lemon juice
1 tablespoon butter
1 tablespoon milk

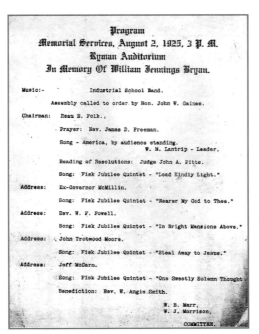

*William Jennings Bryan
appeared at the Tabernacle in
1900, speaking in opposition
to U.S. expansionism. He is
reputed to have later told Lula
Naff that the Tabernacle was
the greatest hall for speaking
in America. He returned to
Tennessee in 1925 as prosecutor
in the famous Scopes evolution
trial, facing Clarence Darrow
for the defense. He won
the case, but the clash was so
stressful that he died a few
days after the trial. A memorial
service was held at the
Ryman with the address given
by Ex-Governor McMillin
and the music provided by the
Fisk Jubilee Quintet.*

Mix the raisins and walnuts in a small bowl. Mix the brown sugar,
flour, lemon peel, cinnamon, mace and salt in a medium bowl. Layer
half the apples in a pastry-lined pie plate and sprinkle with half the
lemon juice. Layer half the raisin mixture and half the brown sugar
mixture over the apples. Repeat the layers and dot with the butter.
Top with the remaining pastry, trimming and sealing the edges. Brush
the top with milk. Bake at 425 degrees for 30 to 45 minutes or until
the apples are tender and the crust is golden brown, covering with
foil if necessary to prevent overbrowning. Serve warm with ice cream.

Yield: 8 servings.

Program courtesy of Nashville Room, Nashville and Davidson County Library

Grilled Fish

If Nashville politicians entertained Alfred Smith on Friday, they might have served him this dish; Smith, who opposed prohibition, was the first Catholic to run for President of the United States.

⅓ cup dry sherry
⅓ cup olive oil
3 tablespoons wine vinegar
Juice of 1 lemon or lime
2 tablespoons soy sauce
2 tablespoons grated fresh ginger
2 cloves of garlic, minced
Peppercorns and oregano to taste
6 (6-ounce) salmon, tuna or mahimahi steaks

Combine the sherry, olive oil, wine vinegar, lemon juice, soy sauce, ginger, garlic, peppercorns and oregano in a shallow dish and mix well. Add the fish, turning to coat well. Marinate in the refrigerator for 6 hours, turning several times. Drain, discarding the marinade. Grill the fish over hot coals until the fish flakes easily, turning occasionally.

Yield: 6 servings.

FROM GRANDMOTHER'S COOKBOOK

To Barbecue Fish

Salt the fish well; put it in a baking-pan nearly full of water and boil until almost done, then pour off most of the water. Have ready a cupful of vinegar, black pepper and Worcestershire sauce and butter, melted together. Pour this over fish, a little at a time, until the fish is done. Sift a little flour over the fish between the times of putting on sauce and it will brown nicely.

The Ryman saw many political occasions over the years, including the inauguration of Governor Austin Peay in 1923. One of the most notable, however, had to be the rousing speech by Alfred E. Smith during the presidential campaign of 1928. So many people attended the event that there was standing room only and many people crowded into the wings to stand behind the curtains. When they discovered that they could neither see nor hear, some of the more daring cut holes in the curtains, which doubtless helped them see, but they reported that they still could not hear the speech.

Prison Bars

Debs would have been glad to see these bars during one of his prison stays.

1 cup raisins
1 cup sugar
1 cup water
½ cup margarine
½ teaspoon nutmeg
1 teaspoon cinnamon
¼ teaspoon salt
2¼ cups flour
½ teaspoon baking powder
1 teaspoon baking soda
½ cup chopped pecans

Combine the raisins, sugar, water, margarine, nutmeg, cinnamon and salt in a saucepan. Bring to a boil and reduce the heat. Simmer for 10 minutes. Cool to room temperature. Sift the flour, baking powder and baking soda together. Add to the cooled mixture and mix well. Stir in the pecans. Spread in a greased baking pan. Bake at 350 degrees for 20 minutes. Cool in the pan on a wire rack. Cut into bars. May frost with confectioners' sugar frosting if desired.

Yield: 4 dozen.

Eugene Debs also drew crowds when he spoke at the Ryman, but he was no more successful in his bid for the presidency than was Al Smith. Debs' refusal to comply with a federal injunction in the Pullman car strike in 1894 and his speech condemning war during World War I had both earned him prison terms. He came out of jail a confirmed socialist and ran for the presidency five times as the candidate for the Socialist Party. His book, Walls and Bars, dealt with prison conditions and problems.

FROM GRANDMOTHER'S COOKBOOK

Walnut Wafers

Beat 1 egg and add 2 cupfuls of brown sugar and 1 1/2 cupfuls of walnuts chopped fine, stir 1 teaspoon of baking powder into 1 cupful of Light Crust flour and add it and a scant 1/2 cupful of sweet milk. Use enough more flour to make a batter that drops easily from the spoon. Drop on a buttered pan by teaspoonfuls some distance apart. Bake in a fairly quick oven (425 degrees).

Fisk University and several local high schools used the Ryman for graduation ceremonies. Nashville's Dr. Emma Louise White Bragg was the valedictorian of her Pearl High School graduating class at the Ryman in 1928. Dr. White is descended from one of the original members of the Fisk Jubilee Singers, who were also regular performers at the Ryman. Hume Fogg High School's graduation at the Ryman in 1923 included Martha White Lindsey, the daughter of Richard Lindsey, founder of Nashville's Royal Flour Mill. Their best-selling flour, named for her, later became a sponsor of the Grand Ole Opry.

Emma Louise White Bragg at her graduation held in the Ryman Auditorium

Italian Parmesan Twists

This recipe is from Martha White's Southern Sampler cookbook and would have been a nice addition to any graduation celebration. Serve the twists with a dipping sauce of tomato sauce seasoned with garlic powder, oregano, thyme and a little Worcestershire sauce.

> 1 cup grated Parmesan cheese
> 1½ teaspoons Italian seasoning
> 1 (8-ounce) package Martha White Deep Pan Pizza Crust Mix
> ⅓ cup melted butter

Combine the Parmesan cheese and Italian seasoning in a shallow plate. Prepare the pizza crust mix using the package directions. Divide into 6 portions and divide each portion into quarters, making 24 pieces. Roll each piece of dough into a 4-inch rope. Dip each rope into the butter and roll in the cheese mixture. Twist each rope 3 times and place on a greased baking sheet.

Bake at 450 degrees for 7 to 9 minutes or until golden brown.

Yield: 2 dozen.

Photograph courtesy of W. G. Thuss and Dr. Emma Bragg

Creme de Menthe Coffee

Amundsen surely looked forward to warming drinks on his Antarctic trip, but probably nothing as special as this.

¾ cup whipping cream
3 tablespoons creme de menthe
2 tablespoons sugar
1 cup water
⅓ cup sugar
6 chocolate mints
¾ cup milk
¾ cup half-and-half
2 cups strong fresh coffee

Beat the whipping cream with the creme de menthe and 2 tablespoons sugar in a chilled mixer bowl at medium speed until soft peaks form. Chill until serving time. Combine the water, ⅓ cup sugar and mints in a saucepan. Heat until the sugar dissolves and the mints melt, stirring to mix well. Stir in the milk and half-and-half. Cook until heated through. Stir in the coffee. Serve hot in mugs topped with the minted whipped cream.

Yield: 6 servings.

The AMPICO---
"the ALL of the Piano"—re-enacts the art of the world's most famous pianists.
Obtainable in the Chickering and the Fischer Pianos.
CLAUDE P. STREET PIANO CO.
"HOME OF THE AMPICO"
168-170 Eighth Ave., N.

Captain Roald Amundsen
Famous Arctic and Antarctic Explorer. Discoverer of the South Pole. Leader of the Recent Airplane Expedition to the North Pole
ILLUSTRATED LECTURE:
"Our Airplane Dash for the North Pole"
Ryman Auditorium, Saturday Evening, Nov. 14, 1925, 8:15 P. M. } Auspices of Nashville Chapter American Association of University Women

HALL & BENEDICT
INSURANCE SERVICE
Nashville Trust Bldg.
A. B. Benedict   T. Graham Hall

Roald Amundsen, the famous Norwegian explorer who discovered the South Pole in 1911, appeared at the Ryman under the auspices of the American Association of University Women. His "illustrated lecture" in 1925, however, was on the exciting subject of "Our Airplane Dash for the North Pole." The audience that night little dreamed that in only one short year adventure would turn to tragedy for Amundsen when he met his death in an effort to rescue Unberto Nobile, the pilot of a dirigible attempting to cross the North Pole.

Lyceums and Chatauquas provided the entertainment demanded by the public, often in the form of speakers. Commodore Matthew Perry, Thomas Dixon, and Alf and Robert Taylor appeared at the Auditorium under their auspices. Later speakers included the suffragist Sylvia Pankhurst, Helen Keller, and aviator Eddie Rickenbacker. Lorado Taft spoke on sculpture and Elbert Hubbard on the roycrofters. Local professors taught everything from ethics to engineering. Sam Jones and Thomas Ryman would have approved when Carrie Nation and Frances Willard used the podium to speak against strong drink.

Mint Punch

Even Carrie Nation would have approved of this refreshing drink, but she won't know if you add a little bourbon.

> 3 oranges
> 6 lemons
> 2½ cups water
> 2 cups sugar
> 1 cup crushed fresh mint leaves

Cut the zest of 2 oranges and 3 lemons into thin strips. Squeeze the juice from all the oranges and lemons. Place the zest and juices in a bowl. Combine the water and sugar in a saucepan. Boil until the sugar is dissolved. Pour over the orange and lemon mixture. Add the mint leaves. Let stand at room temperature for 2 hours. Strain. Dilute the mixture ¼ to ½ strength with water. Serve chilled.

Yield: 6 to 8 servings.

FROM GRANDMOTHER'S COOKBOOK

A Cooling Drink

Pour three quarts of boiling water on an ounce of cream of tartar, stir in the juice of a fresh lemon, and the peel cut off in very thin strips without a particle of pulp, sweeten to your taste with powdered sugar, stir all well together, then let it stand until cold and clear; pour off without disturbing the sediment at the bottom. A tumblerful iced is a pleasant and healthy beverage for a warm summer day.

Morning Eye Opener

This tasty eye opener is slightly less drastic than W. C. Field's prescription and much tastier.

> 1 (40-ounce) can vegetable juice cocktail
> 1 cup vodka
> ¼ cup Worcestershire sauce
> 1 teaspoon Tabasco sauce
> Juice of 3 limes
> ½ teaspoon garlic powder
> Celery salt, salt and pepper to taste

Combine the vegetable juice cocktail, vodka, Worcestershire sauce, Tabasco sauce, lime juice and seasonings in a pitcher and mix well. Chill until serving time. Pour into glasses and garnish with ribs of celery.

Yield: 8 servings.

The other side of the drinking issue also had proponents at the Ryman. The ghosts of Sam Jones and Thomas Ryman must have had an uneasy sleep the night W. C. Fields proclaimed on stage that the best cure for a hangover was the application to the throat and stomach of the juice of three bottles of whiskey.

W. C. Fields

The Boy Scout movement
founded in England in 1907
by Sir Robert Stephenson
Smyth Baden-Powell spread
to the United States in 1909.
Sir Baden-Powell made
several early speaking tours
of the United States in
support of the movement.
His journals in the
National Scouting Museum
indicate that he spoke at
the Ryman Auditorium on
February 23, 1912. It
must have been a fairly
uneventful lecture, for the
journal contains no
other comments on his
Nashville stop.

Beef Kabobs

Sir Baden-Powell's days in the military indicated to him that boys needed more experience in outdoor life. This recipe is one that boys could prepare on an outdoor grill or fire.

1 cup vegetable oil
1 cup wine vinegar
2 teaspoons onion
    powder
2 teaspoons garlic
    powder
1 teaspoon oregano
Salt and pepper to taste
3 pounds lean beef cubes
2 (16-ounce) cans
    whole small potatoes
1 pound mushrooms
2 green bell peppers, cut up
3 onions, cut into wedges
8 pita bread rounds, cut into halves

Sir Baden-Powell, founder of the Boy Scout movement, with his wife and, on the right, Juliette Lowe, founder of the Girl Scout movement

Combine the oil, vinegar, onion powder, garlic powder, oregano, salt and pepper in a sealable plastic bag and mix well. Add the beef. Marinate for several hours; drain. Alternate the beef, potatoes, mushrooms, green peppers and onions on skewers. Cook over hot coals until the beef is cooked through, turning frequently. Serve in pita bread rounds.

Yield: 8 servings.

Photograph courtesy of Girl Scout Council of Cumberland Valley

Mrs. Roosevelt at a reception given by the Girl Scout Council of Nashville on the occasion of her address at the Ryman

Original Girl Scout Cookies

This is the recipe used for the original Girl Scout Cookies. Mrs. Roosevelt would have been surprised at some of the exotic choices available today.

1 cup butter, softened
1 cup sugar
2 eggs, beaten
2 tablespoons milk
1 teaspoon vanilla extract
2 cups flour
2 teaspoons baking powder
½ teaspoon salt
1 cup sugar

Cream the butter and 1 cup sugar in a mixer bowl until light and fluffy. Blend in the eggs, milk and vanilla. Sift the flour, baking powder and salt together. Add to the creamed mixture and mix well. Chill for 1 hour. Roll the dough very thin on a lightly floured surface. Cut into 2-inch circles. Place on a cookie sheet. Bake for 8 to 10 minutes or until light brown. Sprinkle with 1 cup sugar. Remove to a wire rack to cool.

Yield: 6 dozen.

Photograph courtesy of Girl Scout Council of Cumberland Valley

It was twenty–six years after Sir Baden–Powell's visit that Eleanor Roosevelt came to the Ryman to speak on behalf of the Girl Scout Council of Nashville, but the visit was beset with embarrassments. Arrangements had been made for Mrs. Roosevelt to enter the Auditorium by the side door, but she was brought to the main door, where one of the doorkeepers demanded her ticket! She was then taken to her dressing room backstage, but "some man" was occupying it, so she was marched across the stage in front of the audience to stand with the Girl Scouts while the Fisk Singers entertained. Finally, she was allowed to give her address on "The Relationship of the Individual to the Community."

Alexander Woollcott, "The Town Crier" was the voice of America when he appeared at the Ryman on his 1939–1940 lecture tour. The famous journalist and raconteur entertained audiences with his personal recollections and stories, and was reputed to have entertained other audiences with stories of the Ryman and her eccentric manager, Lula Naff, after his appearance there. George Kaufman and Moss Hart made Woollcott's eccentricities famous in the play "The Man Who Came to Dinner."

Boiled New England Dinner

Woollcott would have been glad to be the man who came to this traditional New England dinner. You can omit the marinating step if your market has a brisket which has already been seasoned and marinated.

½ cup wine vinegar
½ cup white vinegar
1 cup water
¼ cup sugar
1 tablespoon pickling spice
1 tablespoon whole cloves
2 teaspoons minced garlic
2 bay leaves
1 (5-pound) boneless
    beef brisket
2 heads cabbage, cut
    into wedges
10 medium potatoes, peeled
10 carrots, peeled

IN PERSON
The Town Crier—
FIRST TRANSCONTINENTAL TOUR
ALEXANDER WOOLLCOTT

Combine the vinegars, water, sugar, pickling spice, cloves, garlic and bay leaves in a large bowl. Add the brisket. Marinate in the refrigerator for 8 hours or longer, turning frequently. Remove the brisket to an 8-quart saucepan and cover with water. Simmer for 4 hours or until tender. Remove to a heatproof platter and keep warm. Add the vegetables to the saucepan. Cook until tender. Slice the beef diagonally across the grain. Serve with the vegetables.

Yield: 10 servings.

Poster courtesy of F. Robinson Collection, Vanderbilt University Library

Sunday Meat Loaf

Will Rogers seldom gave himself airs and would have been proud to sit down to this meat loaf served with mashed potatoes and peas.

½ medium onion, chopped
2 tablespoons vegetable oil
1 egg
1 tablespoon Worcestershire sauce
¼ cup milk
2 pounds ground beef
⅓ cup herb-seasoned stuffing mix
2 tablespoons Dijon mustard
2 tablespoons catsup
½ teaspoon salt

Will Rogers

Sauté the onion in the oil in a skillet until tender; drain. Combine the egg, Worcestershire sauce and milk in a bowl and beat lightly. Add the onion, ground beef, stuffing mix, mustard, catsup and salt and mix well. Pack into a 5x9-inch loaf pan. Bake at 350 degrees for 1 hour or until cooked through. Slice to serve.

Yield: 8 servings.

Audiences at the Ryman loved the popular and down-to-earth Will Rogers, who claimed that all he knew was what he read in the newspapers and that when Washington newspapers said that Congress was deadlocked and couldn't act, he thought it the greatest blessing that could befall the country. Lula Naff appreciated the fact that Rogers always bought the tickets he gave away as complimentary, rather than expecting the Auditorium to donate them. She was exasperated the night of his performance, however, when a large number of physicians attended and received so many noisy pages that she missed some of Rogers' remarks.

Big Mama's Teacakes

Jerry says that "you can eat the dough raw too — it's plumb yellow and good."

1 cup butter, softened
1 cup (heaping) sugar
2 eggs
3 cups flour
1 teaspoon baking soda
½ teaspoon salt
3 tablespoons buttermilk
1 teaspoon vanilla extract
Sugar for sprinkling on the top

Cream the butter and 1 cup sugar in a mixer bowl until light and fluffy. Beat in the eggs. Mix the flour, baking soda and salt together. Add to the creamed mixture alternately with the buttermilk and vanilla, mixing well after each addition. Spoon by tablespoonfuls onto a lightly greased cookie sheet. Sprinkle with additional sugar. Bake at 350 degrees for 8 to 13 minutes or until golden brown.

Yield: 6 dozen.

Humorist Jerry Clower once had an argument with opponents of capital punishment as a deterrent to crime. He told them that "it's very obvious ain't none of y'all ever stole no teacakes from my mama and got caught...I stole two of them big pretty yellow teacakes and...Mama said, 'Jer-ry. Did you steal any of them teacakes?' I said, 'No, ma'am.' Well, about a hour later my mama caught me sitting on my cotton sack eating them teacakes. And when my mama got through with me, I never ever have ever stole another teacake. And I don't eat a cookie now of no kind that I don't call Mama and see if it's all right."

FROM GRANDMOTHER'S COOKBOOK

Tea Cake

1 teaspoon baking powder stirring in part of the flour;
1 heaping cup sugar, 2/3 cup lard; mix lard and sugar then put 1 egg,
1/2 cup sweet milk; flavor to taste.

Brown Sugar Pound Cake

Thanks to Willard Scott for sharing this delicious glazed pound cake recipe.

1 cup butter
½ cup shortening
5 eggs
3¼ cups packed brown sugar
3½ cups flour
½ teaspoon baking powder
1 cup milk
1 cup chopped pecans
½ cup melted butter
1 (1-pound) package confectioners' sugar
Milk

Marty Stuart and
Willard Scott

NBC newsman Willard Scott had a wonderful time clowning around at the Ryman with Marty Stuart, Mandy Barnett and Tere Myers. After his singing session with Marty, however, it was recommended to him that he not give up his day job.

Cream 1 cup butter and shortening in a mixer bowl until light. Beat in the eggs 1 at a time. Add the brown sugar gradually, mixing well. Sift the flour and baking powder together. Add to the batter alternately with 1 cup milk, mixing well after each addition. Spoon into a greased and floured tube pan.

Bake at 325 degrees for 1¼ to 1½ hours or until the cake tests done. Cool in the pan for several minutes. Remove to a serving plate to cool completely. Combine the pecans with ½ cup melted butter in a broiler pan. Place under the broiler and broil until toasted. Cool slightly. Add the confectioner's sugar and enough milk to make of spreading consistency. Spread over the top of the cake, allowing some to drip down the side and over the center.

Yield: 16 servings.

Photograph courtesy of Donnie Beauchamp

Powdermilk Biscuits

Garrison Keillor invented Powdermilk Biscuits as a sponsor for the "Prairie Home Companion" in homage to Martha White, sponsor of the Grand Ole Opry. He reports that on his first visit to the Opry when Lester Flatt and Earl Scruggs and the Foggy Mountain Boys came on for Martha White and cranked up that theme song, it was like the lights went out and the rockets went up. This is our version of a recipe for Powdermilk Biscuits.

1 cup sifted all-purpose flour
1 cup Powdermilk whole wheat flour
1 tablespoon baking powder
¾ teaspoon salt
¾ cup milk
¼ cup vegetable oil

Garrison Keillor returned to the Ryman yet again, when the broadcast of his "Prairie Home Companion" was scheduled as one of the first events to take place in the renovated Ryman Auditorium in June of 1994. The original plan had been for one performance only on Saturday night, June 4, but the response was so great that he consented to perform on the preceding Friday night as well, when he recalled with nostalgia his earlier visits to the Auditorium.

Combine the all-purpose flour, whole wheat flour, baking powder and salt in a bowl. Make a well in the center. Add the milk and oil and stir with a fork just until the dough leaves the side of the bowl. Knead lightly on a floured surface. Roll or pat ½ inch thick. Cut into 2-inch circles. Place on a lightly greased baking sheet.

Bake at 450 degrees for 12 to 15 minutes or until golden brown.

Yield: 1 dozen.

Garrison Keillor and Chet Atkins

Photograph courtesy of Donnie Beauchamp

I remember my first trip to the Opry, driving a night and a day from Minnesota
with a friend, listening to the Friday-night show and getting into Nashville
on Saturday morning to find out that the Saturday-night show was sold out. I
watched my first Opry from the Allright parking lot beside the Ryman, which
was not a bad deal, considering that the Ryman wasn't air-conditioned and
the windows were open wide enough that we could see if we crouched down.
Even from the outside, the Opry had much to recommend it. The music drifted
out — high lonesome voices, sweetened with steel guitars, singing about
being left behind, walked out on, dropped, shunned, shut out, abandoned, and
otherwise mistreated, which a fellow who's driven eight hundred and sixty-one
miles to crouch in a parking lot can really get into.

I was lucky enough to be backstage for the Opry's last performance at the
Ryman. Even before the last show began, the attention that the audience directed at
the stage was intense. By the time Bill Anderson and the Po' Boys came on and
the first notes came out and Grant Turner raised his arms for applause, it seemed as
if the show, which looked small compared with what you'd imagined at home as you
listened to the radio, couldn't bear up under this scrutiny, and would sink from view
under all the passengers onstage. All of us knew that it was something we'd always
remember, yet the harder we looked, the more it slipped away.

So the best place to see the Opry that night, I decided, was in the WSM
control booth with my eyes shut, leaning against the back wall, the music coming
out of the speaker just like radio, that good old AM mono sound. The room
smelled of hot radio tubes, and, closing my eyes, I could see the stage as clearly as
when I was a kid lying in front of our Zenith console. It was good to let the Opry
go out the same way it had first come to me, through the air in the dark. After the
show, it was raining hard, and the last Opry crowd to leave the Ryman ran.

Excerpted from Garrison Keillor's "Onward and Upward with the Arts at the Opry."
New Yorker. May 16, 1974, pp 46–59.

Dolly Parton Soup

This is one of Ned McWherter's favorites, a soup created by his mother Lucille and named by her.

Ned McWherter, Governor of Tennessee from 1987 to 1995, graced the stage of the Ryman on several occasions, notably at its reopening in 1994. His personal memories of his experiences there are quite succinct, however. He says that he "tried to sing; failed. Made campaign speech: elected Governor, 1986." That's probably why that even though he made his name in politics rather than in music, his has been a career leavened with humor.

1 medium head cabbage, chopped
2 large cans chopped tomatoes or fresh tomatoes
1 large can sodium-free tomato juice
4 beef bouillon cubes
2 green bell peppers, chopped
2 medium onions, chopped
1 rib celery, chopped
1 (16-ounce) package frozen okra
5 large carrots, chopped
1 medium can whole kernel corn
1 medium package elbow macaroni

Combine the cabbage, tomatoes, tomato juice and bouillon cubes in a large saucepan. Bring to a boil. Add the green peppers, onions, celery, okra, carrots and corn. Simmer for 30 minutes. Add the macaroni. Simmer for 30 minutes longer.

Yield: 8 servings.

Governor Ned McWherter

At the ribbon-cutting ceremony to reopen the Ryman Auditorium are (left to right) Governor Ned McWherter, Jeanne Pruett, Vice-Mayor David Scobey, Porter Wagoner, Marty Stuart, Little Jimmy Dickens and Hal Ketchum

Special-Occasion Fudge

Porter Wagoner's mother taught him to make this fudge, which he says is so good that you may have to hold a gun on yourself in order to wait until it cools enough to cut and serve.

2 cups sugar
2 tablespoons (heaping) baking cocoa
¼ cup pancake syrup
½ teaspoon salt
Milk
2 tablespoons butter
1 teaspoon vanilla extract
2 tablespoons peanut butter
½ cup chopped English walnuts

Combine the sugar, baking cocoa, syrup and salt in a saucepan. Add just enough milk to make a thick mixture. Bring to a boil. Boil for 4 to 5 minutes or until the sugar is completely dissolved. Remove from the heat and stir in the butter and vanilla. Stir until the mixture begins to cool. Stir in the peanut butter and walnuts. Pour into a large buttered platter. Let stand until cool. Cut into pieces.

Yield: 1¾ pounds.

Photograph courtesy of Donnie Beauchamp

Governor McWherter was also present along with many other dignitaries at the ribbon-cutting ceremonies when the restored Ryman was reopened in June of 1994. Porter Wagoner and Marty Stuart actually held the giant scissors that cut the ribbon to unveil to the public Gaylord Entertainment Company's masterful renovation — one that maintains the character of the old Auditorium in a state-of-the-art facility. The first event staged there was the taping of the television special "The Roots of Country: Nashville Celebrates the Ryman."

Although former Tennessee Governor Lamar Alexander does play the piano and he was seated at the piano on the Ryman stage during his 1995 interview with "Face the Nation," he disclaimed his intention of making his Ryman debut performing. The interview, with Bob Schieffer of CBS, also featured Bob Dole in Washington. At the time both Alexander and Dole were candidates for the Republican presidential nomination and were discussing politics in general and the defeat of the balanced budget amendment in particular. Alexander did take time to point out nationwide that "the old Tabernacle...is about a century old. It's a great place."

Five-Flavor Pound Cake

This is one of the Alexanders' favorite recipes. They give credit for it to Nashville restaurateur, cook and author Miss Daisy, who they say is a great Republican.

1 cup butter or margarine, softened
½ cup shortening
3 cups sugar
5 eggs
3 cups flour
½ teaspoon baking powder
1 cup milk
2 teaspoons lemon extract
2 teaspoons coconut extract
2 teaspoons rum extract
2 teaspoons butter flavoring
2 teaspoons vanilla extract
1 cup sugar
½ cup water

Lamar Alexander

Cream the butter, shortening and 3 cups sugar in a mixer bowl until light and fluffy. Beat the eggs in a small mixer bowl until thick and light yellow. Add to the creamed mixture and mix well. Add a mixture of the flour and baking powder alternately with the milk, mixing well after each addition. Stir in 1 teaspoon of each of the flavorings. Spoon into a greased 10-inch tube pan.

Bake at 325 degrees for 1½ hours or until the cake tests done. Combine the remaining flavorings with 1 cup sugar and the water in a saucepan. Bring to a boil. Pour over the hot cake in the pan. Let stand until cool. Remove to a serving plate.

Yield: 16 servings.

Former secretaries of defense review the American defense policy at the Ryman. Pictured are (left to right): Frank Carlucci, James Schlesinger, Donald Rumsfeld, Moderator Hodding Carter III, Harold Brown, Richard Cheney and Caspar Weinberger.

Risotto con Asparagi

This recipe is shared by Donald Rumsfeld, who served as secretary of defense from 1975 to 1977 under President Gerald Ford.

    5 cups chicken broth
    ⅓ cup finely minced onion
    2 tablespoons unsalted butter
    1 tablespoon vegetable oil
    1½ cups uncooked arborio rice
    ½ cup dry white wine
    12 ounces fresh asparagus, cut into 1-inch pieces
    1 tablespoon unsalted butter
    ¼ cup grated Parmesan cheese

Bring the chicken broth to a simmer in a saucepan and hold at the simmering point. Sauté the onion in 2 tablespoons butter and oil in a saucepan for 1 to 2 minutes, taking care not to brown. Add the rice. Sauté for 1 minute. Stir in the wine. Add the asparagus. Stir in ½ cup of the simmering broth. Cook until the broth is absorbed. Add the remaining broth ½ cup at a time, continuing to cook after each addition until the broth is absorbed, about 18 minutes. Remove from the heat. Stir in 1 tablespoon butter and cheese. Serve immediately.

Yield: 4 servings.

Photograph courtesy of Southern Center for International Studies

In 1995, the Ryman Auditorium was the setting for the taping of the Ninth Annual Report of the Secretaries of Defense, an in-depth review of American Defense Policy produced by the Southern Center for International Studies. It featured U.S. Secretaries of Defense Richard Cheney, Frank Carlucci, Caspar Weinberger, Harold Brown, Donald Rumsfeld and James Schlesinger. The program, with a special focus on Bosnia, was moderated by Hodding Carter III. Of the Ryman, Caspar Weinberger said, "It is a sign of a good civilization for cities to preserve and maintain historic areas such as the Ryman Auditorium."

PROGRAM NOTES

Captain Roald Amundsen

Famous Arctic and Antarctic Explorer.   Discoverer of the South
Pole.   Leader of the Recent Airplane Expedition
to the North Pole

ILLUSTRATED LECTURE:

"Our Airplane Dash for the North Pole"

Ryman Auditorium, Saturday Evening, Nov. 14, 1925, 8:15 P. M.	Auspices of Nashville Chapter American Association of University Women

---

...REFERENCES AND SOURCES, INDEXES, ORDER FORM

References and Sources

Baptist Cook Book. Ladies Aid and Missionary Society, The Baptist Church, Omaha, Texas, 1924.

Batchelder, Ann. *New Delineator Recipes.* The Butterick Publishing Company, 1930.

Dye Van Mol & Lawrence Photograph Archives

Eddy, Nelson. "The Ryman - The Tabernacle Becomes a Shrine." Script for the Ryman Centennial Jubilee. Dye Van Mol & Lawrence, Nashville, Tennessee, May 18, 1992.

Eiland, William U. *Nashville's Mother Church: The History of the Ryman Auditorium.* Opryland USA, 1992.

"Face the Nation" television program transcript. CBS, Washington, D.C., March 5, 1995.

Fisk Club Cookbook. Fisk University Library Special Collections, Nashville, Tennessee.

Francis Robinson Collection of Theater, Music and Dance. Vanderbilt University Library Special Collections, Nashville, Tennessee.

Girl Scout Council of Cumberland Valley, Nashville, Tennessee.

Gospel Music Association Archives, Nashville, Tennessee.

Grand Ole Opry Archives, Nashville, Tennessee.

Grand Ole Opry Collection. Vanderbilt University Special Collections, Nashville, Tennessee.

Grand Ole Opry Picture-History Book. Edited by Jerry Strobel. Gaylord Entertainment Company, Nashville, Tennessee, 1994.

Grand Ole Opry Picture-History Book. Edited by Jerry Strobel. WSM Inc., Nashville, Tennessee, 1982.

Habitat for Humanity. *From Our House to Yours.* Favorite Recipes® Press, Nashville, Tennessee, 1993.

Hagan, Chet. *Grand Ole Opry.* Henry Holt and Company, New York, 1989.

Hinshaw, Jane. *Dig into the Past: The Ryman House Site.* Archaeological Report for Historic Nashville, Inc. and the National Endowment for the Humanities, Nashville, Tennessee, 1981.

Housekeeping in the Blue Grass. The Ladies of the Presbyterian Church of Paris, Kentucky, Robert Clarke & Co., Cincinnati, 1881.

Hurst, Jack. *Nashville's Grand Ole Opry.* Harry N. Abrams, Inc., New York, 1975.

Jeter Smith Dance Collection. Nashville Room, Nashville and Davidson County Public Library.

Keillor, Garrison. "Onward and Upward with the Arts at the Opry." *New Yorker.* May 6, 1974, pp. 46-59.

Light Crust Recipes. Burris Mill & Elevator Co., Fort Worth, Texas.

Martha Whites' Southern Sampler. Rutledge Hill Press, Nashville, Tennessee, 1989.

McKeon, Elizabeth. *Elvis in Hollywood: Recipes Fit For a King™.* Rutledge Hill Press, Nashville, Tennessee, 1994.

Metropolitan Opera Archives, New York, New York.

Minnie Pearl. *Minnie Pearl Cooks.* Nashville, Tennessee, 1970.

Norman, Jack. *The Nashville I Knew.* Nashville: Rutledge Hill Press, 1984, pp. 56-57.

Paul, Sara T. *Cookery from Experience.*

Ryman Auditorium Archives.

Sam P. Jones Papers. Hargrett Rare Book and Manuscript Library, University of Georgia Libraries, Athens, Georgia.

Stories from Home. Jerry Clower. University Press of Mississippi, Jackson, Mississippi, 1992.

Southern Center for International Studies, Atlanta, Georgia.

Tennessee State Library and Archives, Nashville, Tennessee.

The First Texas Cook Book. The Pemberton Press, Austin, Texas, 1883.

The Naff Collection. Nashville Room, Nashville and Davidson County Public Library.

The Tennessean/Nashville Banner, Nashville, Tennessee.

Index

Recipe Index

For additional copies

Call 1-800-358-0560

VISA or MasterCard accepted
or send check or money order for

$19.95 per book plus local sales tax and
$3.00 shipping and handling for first book
($.50 for each additional book)

to

FRP™
2451 Atrium Way
Nashville, Tennessee 37214